STORMTROOPER

MILITARY
ILLUSTRATED

STORMTROOPER
ELITE GERMAN ASSAULT SOLDIERS
WRITTEN BY STEPHEN BULL

COLOUR PLATES BY RICHARD HOOK
SERIES EDITOR TIM NEWARK

Current titles
Marine
Stormtrooper
Rifleman
Highlander

Future titles
Ranger
Paratrooper
Legionary
Samurai

First published in 1999 in Great Britain
by Publishing News Ltd

UK editorial office:
Military Illustrated, 39 Store Street,
London WC1E 7DB, Great Britain

Stephen Bull has asserted his moral right to be
identified as the author of this work.

ISBN 1-903040-01-9

Designed by Glenn Howard, Atelier Works

Printed and bound in Singapore under
the supervision of M.R.M. Graphics Ltd,
Winslow, Buckinghamshire

CONTENTS

BIRTH OF THE STORMTROOPER

Opposite, the beginnings
of *Stosstrupptaktik*, 1915.
This bomber has discarded
all heavy equipment and
one of his cartridge carriers,
having a slung rifle and
four grenades for trench
to trench action. Note how
a grenade is held in each
hand and two more are
suspended by their belt
hooks. *SB*

The German Stormtrooper was never a single category of soldier, but an idea, an ethos, which came both to symbolise a revolution in infantry tactics and to strike terror into the enemy. So seductive did the concept become that it would be hijacked for political and propaganda ends, the Stormtrooper being identified as the standard bearer of struggle, and as the guardian and propagator of a revolutionary ideology. The National Socialist 'political' Stormtrooper became the antithesis of the Red Guard and the Communist revolutionary.

Yet the Stormtrooper did not materialise overnight, nor was the the idea of an aggressive, modern, committed, self reliant soldier operating in small integrated groups a purely German phenomenon. The concept was forged in the fire of war, and evolved over a period of years, during which the invention of new weapons and experiments with minor tactics, aimed primarily at breaking the deadlock of the trenches, carried on apace. The genesis of the Stormtrooper was therefore a complex process, with an idea here being gleaned from the French, a weapon there being copied from the British, and all parts synthesised into the new techniques. 'Infiltration' was only part of the picture: Stormtroopers learned how to integrate their weapons systems, support their comrades, and survive as small groups. In short to fight as platoons, or squads, or even as thinking individuals. A few of the new tactics would be instigated by the General Staff and would trickle down the organisation – but very often the process would work in reverse. The *Frontschweine* would discover pragmatically that using a particular technique succeeded, and that another led to a premature death.

The Stormtrooper became regarded as an élite, but this was never the point of the matter: new tactics were tried by experimental units, or first carried into action by special *Sturmbatallione*, but ultimately it was intended that all should learn and profit from the new methods, being retrained and re-equipped as necessary. This was never entirely achieved, nor could it be, because it was an ongoing process. Even during the Second World War, when the term Stormtrooper was itself redefined, the process would be continued by the inception of new weapons and new specialisms. Yet small unit tactics, and the idea of the *Gruppe* or squad would remain crucial.

Arguably Assault Engineers, *Panzergrenadiers*, assault infantry and even the *Volksgrenadiers* were the natural successors of the original Stormtrooper. With the invention of 'Storm' or assault rifles, and the widespread use of sub machine guns and hand-held anti-tank weapons, the idea of the thinking, and tactically self reliant soldier reached its natural conclusion. Eventually indeed half trained troops armed with rocket launchers and automatic weapons, lacking air and armour support, would be expected to do the work of all arms. Such was the importance of the *Sturmtrupp* idea.

FORGED IN THE STORM OF STEEL

Europe had been at peace for forty years when in the summer of 1914, the economic and Imperial rivalries which had created the Entente and the Triple Alliance finally brought the Continent to the brink of war. Frightened of encirclement, and worried by the demographic and economic implications of fighting France and Russia on two fronts, Germany committed the bulk of her army to an aggressive pre-emptive strike through Belgium, in accordance with the plans first formulated by former Chief of the General Staff, Alfred von Schlieffen. The immediate intention was to use seven armies in a massive concentric swing to knock out France, the old enemy of 1870, leaving Austria and Germany to crush the Romanov Empire of Russia at their leisure.

The instrument of victory was to be the Imperial German army: a surprisingly supple amalgam of the

traditional and the modern. Though Kaiser Wilhelm was its titular head, the most important decision maker was the Chief of the General Staff. During the First World War, the General Staff would exercise command through the newly created Supreme Army Command or *Oberste Heeresleitung* (OHL). The army still showed its diverse origins, for though the Prussian force was undoubtedly the core, individual states retained many local distinctions. These included not only details of uniform and tradition, but at least in the case of the Bavarians and Saxons, distinct Army Corps, and for the Bavarians uniquely, a separate numbering system for her regiments. Many

formations retained local titles redolent of past glories: some of the best known made up the Prussian *Garde*, others like Saxon *Leib Grenadier-Regiment Nr 100*, or *Baden Leib-Dragoner Regiment Nr 20*, were the successors to the senior regiments of the smaller states.

The German army operated a system of short service conscription which meant that troops served with the active regular regiments for two or three years, following which they became reservists, liable to annual training and rapid recall to the colours of the Reserve regiments in war. After this, men passed on to the *Landwehr* with a reduced liability, and finally the *Landsturm* in which

Early success in the East: Russian prisoners under guard. Note the Tragegurte or ammunition bandoliers worn around the necks of some of the German infantrymen. *SB*

much of the physically able adult male population up to the age of 45 would be obliged to participate in case of emergency. The advantages of such a system were immediately apparent, for it has been calculated that about two thirds of German soldiers who participated in the Great War had seen some military service prior to 1914. Much retraining was needed during the war, but it proved possible to call up vast numbers very quickly, so that during 1914 the strength of the army in the field leapt from less than one to five million, and later achieved more than six million.

The artillery arm, whose worth had been more than amply proved in the Franco-Prussian war, was now predominantly armed with modern 77mm quick firers backed by a more generous allowance of howitzers and heavy weapons than most other armies. The cavalry was well mounted and was now generally equipped with lances as well as swords and carbines, and the *Ulanen* and *Hussaren* in particular had considerable historic reputations. Nevertheless it was the infantry which bulked largest, and bore the principal burden.

The vast majority of foot soldiers were armed with Mauser rifles and organised into three battalion regiments. Each battalion, totalling 1076 officers and men, was composed of four companies, and each regiment had an extra company for its six machine guns. Though platoons were divided into half platoons or *Halbzüge*, and these themselves were divided into two 16 man *Korporalschaften*, commanded by an *Unteroffizier*, the small subdivisions had little battlefield significance, being essentially groupings for administrative, billeting, and disciplinary purposes. *Jäger*, or light infantry, were originally formed as single battalions, each of four companies and a machine gun company.

As the pre-war Field Regulations observed:

'Infantry is the primary weapon. In tandem with artillery, its fire will batter the enemy. It alone breaks his last resistance. It carries the brunt of combat and makes the greatest sacrifices. Consequently it garners the greatest glory. Infantry must nurture its intrinsic drive to attack aggressively. Its actions must be dominated by one thought: forward against the enemy, cost what may !' As tactician Wilhelm Balck observed just prior to the war, it was the infantry company which was 'the smallest element of a body of troops capable of sustaining an action independently, or performing a simple combat task'.

The traditional formation was close order columns; a disposition which had served well for battlefield march and manoeuvre throughout the nineteenth century, and was still current in the drill regulations of 1888. Remarkably, company 'columns of platoons' were still current in 1914. In this formation each platoon of the company was arranged in a two deep line almost shoulder to shoulder, with the company commander to the fore and the platoons one behind another. When thus arrayed the company was compact enough for the commander to maintain voice control, and for almost every man to be within physical reach of an NCO. Ideally the company advanced in this body until close enough to engage in the firefight, at which point the commander ordered his men into a thick firing line two or three hundred metres in length, which could later charge home or go to ground as the tactical necessity demanded. Ideally one or more companies would engage the enemy

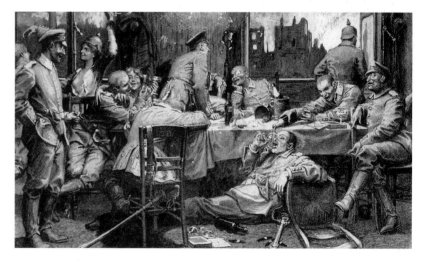

'The orgy', a French view of German troops' behaviour in occupied territory in the Great War. Attempts at 'correctness' were badly marred by wholesale execution of real or suspected spies and franc tireurs. Early Allied atrocity propaganda would, however, backfire, first because some of the stories circulated in 1914 were proved to be fabrications, later because very real massacres perpetrated in the Second World War were not believed. *SB*

frontally, perhaps supplemented by a support line, then the decisive attack would be delivered by the main reserve to a flank.

The relevance of columns and thick lines to modern war, dominated by magazine rifles and machine guns, was questioned in the early years of the century in the aftermath of the South African war. The result was an experiment with 'Boer' tactics, and the 1902 summer manoeuvres saw mock battles in which troops crawled towards their enemies and fought in more open formations. Acceptance of these practices was patchy since in the absence of actual firefights, the efficacy of 'Boer' tactics was difficult to determine empirically, moreover the manoeuvres did demonstrate the difficulties of command which had always been suspected. A further round of tactical debate ensued after the Russo-Japanese war of 1904, in which the Japanese quite unexpectedly trounced their opponents.This result sent mixed messages to German tacticians, for on the one hand the Japanese had worked on German lines and had German advisors. On the other side of the coin it was clear that despite their success the Japanese had taken heavy losses and had adopted looser formations as a result.

So it was that the new drill regulations of 1906 attempted to synthesise the ease of command and the close combat shock value of columns with the devastating effect of rifle fire. According to the text book, the infantry would advance in columns until within about a thousand metres of the enemy, whilst the artillery opened a rapid bombardment. If the shelling suppressed or broke the opposition the columns would surge onward; if it did not, the columns would break down into platoons or half platoons and form a fire line about 500 metres from the enemy. After a brisk fire fight to gain superiority, preferably under the direct control of officers and NCOs, the fire line would rush forward with bayonets fixed and take the position. That this was a more flexible open scheme that would require more of the individual soldier was widely recognised, and the Field Service Regulations, or *Felddienst Ordnung*, of 1908 included the use of tactical exercises for NCOs. So it was that under certain circumstances Sergeants would be expected to give a tactical lead to half platoons or sections in the assault.

In battle the mixed scheme of columns, thick lines, fire fights and rushes, which had been learned better by some than others, met with widely divergent results. Sometimes, especially when facing shaky opposition in open country on the Eastern Front, the German divisions swept all before them. Yet it was noticeable that the denser the formation used the higher the casualties. In one attack, mounted by 43rd Infantry Brigade against the Russians at Gerdauen in East Prussia, sixteen companies were thrown against the enemy. There were relatively light losses, and of these the majority were in the one company which had neglected to advance in open order. In the Argonne, 5th Company of the *König Wilhelm I (6. Württembergisches) Infanterie-Regiment Nr 124*, suffered disaster when two squads, still in column, were completely wiped out by a single shell. This was a particular tragedy since, as Leutnant Erwin Rommel observed, many of their comrades were already operating in skirmish lines

Men of 4. *Magdeburgisches Infanterie-Regiment Nr 67* in full marching order, Münster 1914. All wear field grey uniforms except for the sword carrying NCO in the centre, who sports the *Dunkleblau* dress uniform. The NCO on the left of the group wears the marksman's lanyard, and the unit's G 98 rifles are piled in the foreground. *SB*

with four paces between each man.

On occasions, particularly when met by determined French troops in numbers, or British regulars dug in giving rapid fire, the result of the early style infantry attacks could be catastrophe. As Captain Harry Dillon, 2nd Battalion the Oxford and Buckinghamshire Light Infantry, recorded when facing the onslaught of the *Furor Teutonicus* in October 1914: 'It came with a great suddenness that was the most startling thing I have ever known. A great grey mass of humanity was charging, running for all God would let them, straight on to us from not 50 yards off. Everybody's nerves were pretty well on edge as I had warned them what to expect, and as I fired my rifle the rest went off almost simultaneously. One saw the great mass of Germans quiver. In reality some fell, some fell over them, and others came on. I have never shot so much in such a short time, could not have been more than a few seconds and they were down.

'Then the whole lot came on again and it was the most critical moment of my life. Twenty yards more and they would have been over us in thousands, but our fire must have been fearful, and at the last moment they did the most foolish thing they could possibly have done. Some of the leading people turned left for some reason, and they followed like a great flock of sheep. I don't think one could have missed at the distance and for just one short minute or two we poured the ammunition into them in boxfuls. My rifles were red hot at the finish. The firing died down and out of the darkness a great moan came...'

From the German side of the line, the infantry attacks of 1914 were by turns uplifting, devastating, and confusing. Just one description of many was written by Hauptmann von Brandis of the *Brandenburg Infanterie-Regiment Großherzog Friedrich Franz Nr 24*, recounting the assault on the village of Frameries. It began as planned with a stream of gun and howitzer shells hurtling over the attackers' heads and bursting on the edge of the village. At seven in the morning, six companies went in to the attack, yet the English were not 'Storm ripe', as von Brandis put it, and met the attack with devastating well aimed fire. There were shouts of '*Vorwärts!*' but there were just too many men down to maintain the momentum. The regiment's casualties totalled about half the officers, including three company commanders, and about a third of the rank and file. Regiment *Friedrich Karl von Preußen Nr 64*, taking part in the same attack, reported losses of about a quarter. The village was later taken, but von Brandis was given pause for thought, considering that this tactical debacle had arisen mainly because of the

The German soldier, c 1914. At the outbreak of war, the emphasis was on drill, rifle fire, and bayonet fighting. Heavy casualties and the failure of the old tactics against trench lines would help lead to the evolution both of Stormtroop tactics and new weapons and equipment. *SB*

British recent experience of 'tricks of the trade' in 'small wars'.

Many men had no conception of the power of a modern high velocity fully jacketed, pointed, or *Spitzgeschosse* rifle bullet until it actually hit them. Ulrich Timm, hitherto a Rostock theology student, was shot during fighting at Merkem near Dixmuide. He had just crossed a trench and was advancing with the bayonet in an attack on the rise beyond when 'seized by some irresistible force' and hurled to the ground. With blood running out of his trousers he succeeded in making the slight cover of a hay stack. On examination it was determined that,

'The bullet came from the right front, went first through my right leg, then through the left leg, and finally through my pocket, which was stuffed with fifty field post cards, my New Testament, your last letter, my pay book, and a lot of other small books. Through all this the bullet went, so it must have been travelling with considerable velocity. The wounds only hurt badly during the first few hours...'

Since a British rifle bullet was capable of penetrating nine inches of brick, Timm was very lucky this time: two days later he was found and rescued. In Galicia a few months later he would be less fortunate. Bad though the rifle bullet was it was usually less disfiguring than the shell. Hugo Müller, fighting on the Ancre, recorded how it was necessary to scrape up the brains of his platoon corporal with an entrenching tool after a shell took his head off. He was moved to reflect that most men were becoming more or less callous to the war, since this was preferable to madness.

Adolf Hitler, then serving in the ranks with Bavarian *Reserve-Infanterie Regiment Nr 16*, left a highly evocative account of an attack. He recalled marching on the enemy during a misty autumn Flanders night when suddenly: 'an iron greeting came whizzing at us over our heads, and with a sharp report sent the little pellets flying between

Artillery, machine guns, and solid lines of trenches were major factors in the stalemate which emerged at the end of 1914. Soldiers in fatigue dress march away from freshly dug *Schützengraben* or fire trenches. *SB*

our ranks, ripping up the wet ground: but even before the little cloud had passed, from two hundred throats the first hurrah arose to meet the first messenger of death. Then a crackling and a roaring, a singing and a howling began, and with feverish eyes each one of us was drawn forward, faster and faster, until suddenly past turnip fields and hedges the fight began, the fight of man against man. And from a distance the strains of a song reached our ears... just as death plunged a busy hand into our ranks... "*Deutschland, Deutschland über alles, über alles in der Welt*"'.

The regimental history had it that the singing was not so much a show of patriotic fervour, as a recognition signal to avoid being shot by fellow Germans. The tune identified was *Die Wacht am Rhein*. Thus was born the legend of Langemarck, which would be referred to in popular literature as the Kindermord, or 'Massacre of the Innocents' due to the significant proportion of students and young volunteers in the Reserve Divisions newly committed to battle. The effect on those, like philosophy student Alfred Buchalski, who had gone to war with enthusiasm and 'the natural craving of youth for excitement and experience' was shocking. As he put it, it was not just the casualties, nor the fact that one was occasionally fired on by ones' compatriots which was appalling, but 'the whole way in which a battle is fought is so revolting. To want to fight and not even to be able to defend oneself ! The attack, which I thought was going to be so magnificent, meant nothing but being forced to get forward from one bit of cover to another in the face of a hail of bullets, and not to see the enemy who was firing them'.

It was true that although the performance of the German infantry in 1914 became the stuff of myth it was often tactically inept. As Captain C.J. Paterson of the South Wales Borderers put it, they came on 'in great masses, silly idiots', and there was speculation that these levels of loss simply could not be sustained. Even as late as January 1915,

there were still close order attacks, like that recorded by Adolf Witte on the Eastern Front, in which the men were expected to advance not just shoulder to shoulder, but with their uniform 'cloth touching'. Cynics speculated that this might be so that no Russian bullet should 'have a chance to get past us'.

With the digging of temporary individual scrapes, and then lines of trenches, the problem of the assault was compounded, for not only did the defenders have the advantage of cover, but machine guns and artillery could be set up to fire on predetermined positions locking the front more solidly than ever. Moreover once the front was static, with trenches stretching as far as the eye could see, the defender had no flanks. Machine guns set up at an angle to the main line of defence created enfilades, and the attackers themselves were likely to be outflanked. War became what Robert Otto Marcus, fighting in the Argonne, called 'abominable, cruel, wholesale assassination': a war unworthy of human beings, waged by weapons out of the dark ages, trench mortars, bombs, and flamethrowers. For the defenders, however, it was usually a case of 'sweat saves blood', as the saying put it, – holes in the ground saving lives.

Some, like Hans Martens, just felt helpless; the war had become 'mechanical' a trade of 'systematic manslaughter'. For him, the worst thing of all was the trench mortar: 'They fire noiselessly and a single one often kills as many as 30 men. One stands in the trench, and at any moment a thing like that may burst. The only consolation when one sees the awful explosion made by ours, which is so terrific that sometimes fragments fly back as far as our own parapet, is that... our productions are more effective than those of the French.'

The front line soldier now found himself more than ever a mere pawn in the game of war. When not committed to the attack his life was likely to be circumscribed by what the Germans called the Siegfried dug out; a hole for one or two hollowed

Next page, front line *Schützengraben*. Steel helmets, plentiful supplies of hand grenades, and ammunition bandoliers are kept on the sandbagged fire step.

out under the lip of the trench, supported by a piece of corrugated iron and covered by no more than a couple of metres of earth. Living in a hole in the ground was viewed as vastly preferable to having one's brain pan 'sliced like a cabbage stalk', as Ernst Jünger put it. Yet, though the war was soon static, the ingenuity of men's minds was far from stifled.

SHOCK TROOPS

One of the greatest misconceptions about the First World War is that there were few tactical innovations, until in the last few months of the war 'Stormtroops' suddenly appeared, taking all by surprise. In fact, and as commonsense might suggest, massive casualties and failure on the battlefield soon set minds to work on both sides. The shock of August and September 1914 led to immediate instructions for the use of dispersed formations, but many other suggestions came not from the General Staff but the fighting troops. It was true that many of the innovations met with disaster, but there were ideas aplenty, and the German infantry was in the forefront of experiment.

One possibility, considered even before the outbreak of war, was to advance behind metal shields. This was tried again, but weight, lack of speed, and cost made them impractical on all but a very limited basis. In December 1914, the *Garde*

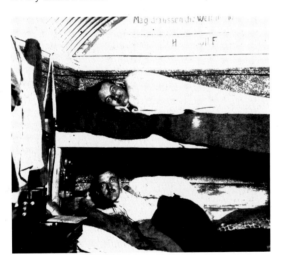

Right, dispersed deep dugouts made sure that at least a proportion of the trench garrison survived to fight off Allied attack. *SB*

Schützen were involved in a minor attack in the Vosges: the battalion commander Major von Hadeln decided against a frontal attack, and instead succeeded in approaching the French trench from either end, from parts of the line which the enemy had previously broken through and apparently bypassed. Using just parts of two companies, one of them led by Hauptmann Willy Rohr, the daring night attack drove the French out with minimal loss. In February 1915, *Fahnrich* August Hopp was tasked with leading an assault party of volunteers into the French trenches: he failed, but the attempt was instructive for he sought out the remains of an old communication trench and approached in file, rather than going 'over the top' in line.

The words *Stosstrupp*, and *Stosstrupptakik*, meaning 'shock troop' and 'shock troop tactics' were soon in use, and were commonly understood to refer to the use of small groups of men attacking the enemy, with whatever weapons, in non-standard formations. A precise definition is difficult, however, since the actual fighting methods were in a state of constant evolution. Yet arguably the development of all these associated minor tactics represented a move away from the application of pure firepower, or *Feuerkraft*, towards *Stosskraft* or assault power. So it was that there was a move away from linear formations, good for the application of rifle fire, and towards more flexible nonlinear formations, whose force was applied by means of *Nahkampfmittel* or the weapons of close combat, grenade, pistol, knife and bayonet. It has been claimed that the word *Stosstruppen*, 'shock troops', was first coined by Major Hermann Reddemann, the former Leipzig fire chief who came to command the flamethrowers of the *Garde-Reserve-Pionier Bataillon*. This may be true, but it is certainly not the case that *Stosstrupptaktik* or Stormtroop tactics sprang ready made from the mind of any one individual.

With the enemy now concealed behind parapets it was generally apparent that weapons capable of being propelled overhead were at a premium.

Opposite, the MG 08 in the front line fire trenches, 1914-1915. The gunner uses the ZF 12 optical sight; other members of the crew are equipped with leather dragging straps. Later in the war the heavy MG 08, which was accurate over long ranges, was moved further back to second line trenches and rear areas, being replaced by light machine guns for close work. *SB*

Over the page, Stormtroop Attack, Western Front, 1918. The forward units of an assault division are depicted attacking from left to right across the battlefield. Continuous trench lines are to be seen in the corners of the picture, but the German *Vorfeldzone*, or outpost zone, actually consisted of nests located in concrete bunkers, improved shell holes, and ruins which ran between the main lines of resistance. Stormtroop detachments would have been hidden here over night,

prior to a morning assault. A typical two man sniper and observer team cover a sector near to the large concrete machine gun position.

Top right, a combined grenadier and light machine gun *Stosstrupp* is making good progress through the British line, advancing under covering fire from their *MG08/15*. The leaders attack boldly, largely ignoring any resistance to either side of them, and push on into their own barrage of gas and high explosive shells which is dropping onto the enemy

second line. These troops wear their gas masks, and carry grenade bags and carbines. Top centre, an NCO armed with a semi-automatic pistol directs a detachment tasked with rolling up the British front line trench. This group is reinforced with the company MP18 sub-machine guns, and a light flamethrower for use against bunkers.

Despite the close support of a man hauled infantry gun, the attack of the *Kampfzug* or battle platoon, bottom right, has been

The result was a massive demand for grenades, trench mortars, catapults, and finally gas. As far as grenades were concerned, new tactics, training, and formations were immediately evolved to match the new conditions. Leutnant Beumelburg of *Pionier Bataillon 30* was credited with the invention of a method subsequently known as *Aufrollen*, the 'rolling up' of enemy trenches by bombing along them. Although he may indeed have been the first to inject theory into the system, the idea of bombing along trenches seems to have quickly taken hold in many places hindered only by the early lack of suitable grenades. The result was that improvisation took up where the commissariat left off, and many troops followed the instruction of officers at local level making up crude bombs from tin cans, lumps of explosive, and wooden handles to supplement the inadequate issues of the time fused ball and 'explode on impact' discus grenades. Many of the improvised grenades had to be lit manually before being thrown: old hands therefore learned to go into battle with a lit cigar in their mouths, which was easier to manipulate than matches or strikers.

Soon it became common to front any attack with bomb throwers, often drawn from the Pioneers, as was recorded by Walter Ambroselli when facing the French near Fort Condé in mid January 1915. The attack in which he participated was signalled at 12, followed by which came, 'a deafening "Hurrah!", and we were off each man running as hard as he could with bayonet lowered, through the French wire entanglements and into the first French trench. There we found only one or two scared Frenchmen in the few dug outs which had not been destroyed by our shells and trench mortars. They instantly threw down their arms. Meanwhile, however, the French machine guns were mowing down our ranks appallingly. They had nearly all been moved back into the second line and were firing on us from

stalled by a combination of uncut wire, and British troops who man the fire step. The Stormtroops attempt to force a passage with long handled wire cutters and Bangalore torpedoes, whilst bombs are hurled over the obstacle. A messenger dog brings grenades to men who have taken refuge in shell holes. The losses in this sector are serious: for despite the success of the new tactics in achieving breakthroughs these still had to be paid for in blood. The year 1918 cost the German army approxi-

mately 1.6 million casualties of whom 380,000 were killed.

The main body of the infantry has been held in reserve, but is now leaving the trenches to the left of the picture having used short ladders, foot holds cut into the trench walls, and specially constructed sap heads for the purpose. Led by their company commanders, they will form a rough skirmish line which will take advantage of any cover, and gaps created by the shock troops. These men carry rifles with fixed bayonets and improvised

assault packs, some have ammunition boxes, others spades and sandbags for improving their final positions which are intended to be on the Allied artillery lines. Welcome additions to firepower include some semi-automatic pistols, and a captured Lewis gun carried by a man near the trench bridge.

The German trenches are now manned by only a skeleton garrison, including a few observers, a sentry wearing trench armour, and a *Granatenwerfer* team,

far left. Nearby battalion stretcher bearers bring a wounded man back to the front line dressing station. Local overhead cover is provided by *Siegfried* shelters cut under the forward lip of some of the trenches, but there are also deeper bunkers for weapons crews and headquarters. Bottom left are a 17cm medium *Minenwerfer* manned by Pioneers, and an MG08. Both are in pits, the latter has been pintle mounted and fitted with a ring sight for anti-aircraft defence over

the battle zone. It should be observed that for reasons of space, distances have been contracted in this illustration: a main line of resistance could be anything up to a kilometre behind the outpost zone; further battle and reserve lines could be located three to four kilometres to the rear.
Painting by Richard Hook

there. However, they did not stop us... our Pioneers, who are more feared than anybody because of their bombs, worked with axes and wire cutters in front of and among us, and just then I witnessed, with admiration, a heroic deed. A Pioneer caught sight of a Frenchman in the trench who was about to fire. The Pioneer quickly pulled the stopper out of the fuse, raised his bomb, and was just going to throw it. At that very moment some German comrades came between him and his objective. He could not throw the bomb without hitting them ; so he kept it in his hand, and in a few seconds it exploded, blowing him to pieces.

'From the second trench we went across a field. All about dead and wounded were lying. The clay stuck to our bodies, especially our hands and feet so that we could hardly get along. I saw some men running bare foot, their boots having got stuck in the mud. Our ranks kept getting thinner... Many ghastly things happened... It makes me sick to think of them.'

Later in 1915, matters were formalised enough for manuals to be issued giving details of small unit grenade tactics for the infantry as a whole. The basic unit specified was the Handgranatentrupp of six to eight men: these were selected from their parent unit on the basis of their courage and skill with bombs. They were entitled to the use of

A machine gun team using an MG 08 on an improvised trench mount. Expedients such as this improved mobility prior to the widespread introduction of light machine guns.

distinctive badges, which, from the latter part of the year onward, appear often to have taken the form of a simple stick grenade shape worn on the upper sleeve. In defence, the bombing groups were positioned in the centre of their infantry platoon, ready to launch small scale counter attacks against enemy troops who penetrated the trench system. Grenades were placed in readiness at selected points in the line, and in defensive posts, boxes for bombs were actually built into the wall of the trench.

In the event of the opposition gaining a lodgement in a German trench, the *Handgranatentrupp* were instructed, without waiting for orders, to: 'immediately attack the enemy with grenades before it becomes necessary to erect a barricade in the trench. On a signal from their commander the men of the bombing party are to equip themselves with hand grenades and collect around him.

'All men of the party carry their rifles slung, bayonets fixed and daggers ready, with the exception of the two leaders who do not carry rifles. The latter may carry as many grenades as they can conveniently handle and should, if possible, be armed with pistols. The commander, similarly armed, follows the two leading men. If no pistols are available, the commander, who should cover the two leading men, carries his rifle ready loaded in his hands. The remaining three men follow the others one traverse to the rear; they keep within sight of their commander, and carry as many grenades as possible. When possible the grenades are carried in their boxes. The two leading men advance along the trench in a crouching posture, so that the commander can fire over them.

'The interval between traverses is crossed at a rush... If the enemy has penetrated into the trench with a large force, and a continuation of his attack is to be expected, as good a barricade as the circumstances permit should be erected. The bombing party should at first remain on the defensive behind this barricade or breastwork.

Rifles should be unslung ready for use. The commander and the rear three men should take up position behind the nearest traverse and within sight of the two leading men. Bombing parties belonging to the platoons in support and in reserve should be stationed somewhere in the vicinity of the communication trenches, and should be brought up to the strength of eight men including the commander.'

In the attack, the *Handgranatentrupp* was intended to lead the way down the enemy trenches, rather than out along the top. Further refinements, introduced in 1916, saw the grenade squad increased to nine including the commander, and subdivided into two subsections of four. The cutting edge was the first subsection of the *Gruppe*, armed with six bombs each plus pistols and trench knives. Two of these were picked bomb throwers, and two carriers in close support. Sudden showers of grenades could be provided by all four throwing in concert. The rear subsection was made up of carriers and spare men. Ideally these were equipped with rifle and bayonet, six grenades, and 25 empty sandbags secured by their haversack straps.

Instructions from 1916 saw the party advance along the trenches well spread out so as to minimise casualties from enemy bombing.

Assault troops in a shell hole. The men are lightly equipped but carry grenade bags and entrenching tools in improvised carriers at the waist; their helmets are camouflaged with mud. Note the rank buttons on the collar of the pipe smoking NCO.

Traverses were to be 'bombed over'; and the 'number two' in the group was to call out 'Geraümt! meaning 'cleared !' to the leader as each was taken. The leader would then give the order to advance. In some instances the squad leader was provided with small white marker flags to be placed at intervals on the traverses to prevent friendly squads from attacking each other. If the advance of the party was completely halted by determined resistance, a barricade was erected across the trench to hold the ground already taken. On the command 'Sändsache vor!' (sandbags forward!) the rear members of the squad set to work to build a blockade; usually between the two subsections of the group. The forward subsection could thus concentrate on defence. Individual machine gun posts or blockhouses required slightly different tactics. Here one or two members of the group would be detailed to take up sniping positions, firing on the loopholes of the objective. The rest would attempt to work around the flanks and rear making use of shell holes and terrain. Finally they would rush the position, bombing it

The 'heroes bunker' on Hill 151, built in June 1917 for the headquarters of first battalion Infanterie-Regiment Nr 422. A good illustration of how individual posts could be protected against all but a direct hit from the heaviest guns by means of layers of logs, concrete, and sand. German engineers would also pioneer the use of reinforced concrete on the Western Front. SB

into submission from unexpected angles.

An interesting technical innovation of 1916 was the combined use of small 'Eier' or egg grenades with stick bombs. In this case one of the members of the forward subsection would be armed with stick grenades for the usual close range work, another would throw the smaller missiles to longer ranges attempting to interfere with the enemy efforts to resupply their own grenadiers. By this means the chances of demoralising the enemy before they got close, or of winning the close range duel were increased. Consistent supply of bombs to the German grenade parties was itself a critical matter. According to published theory it was intended that the throwers should obtain immediate supplies from the men behind them, reserving their own for emergency use. The whole attacking party was itself to be replenished from the rear by its parent unit; a handy method being sandbags containing half a dozen bombs each being passed forward. Occasionally messenger dogs were used to carry bombs by means of a canine grenade waistcoat.

To train the new bombing tactics a special area known as the Handgranatenstand was set aside. Where possible this was laid out so as to mimic actual battlefield conditions, with trenches, wire, loopholes and sapheads. Initially volunteers were sought for the programmes, but as the war continued and the importance of bombs was recognised attendance became general. The training itself was of two types, theoretical, and practical. The first consisted of lectures on grenade types and mechanisms, the latter of actual throwing and squad practices. Much of the initial work was carried out with dummy bombs which were painted red. These included both stick types, which had special cast iron heads of approximately the right weight and were often drilled through to make them obvious, and dummy disc and egg bombs which were sometimes included in the consignments of live bombs.

Later, fused practice bombs lacking their main charge were used: finally came live bombs. Safety and deliberation were paramount. Men were taught to pick up bombs with their throwing hand rather than change from hand to hand and risk a fumble. They were to take their time but not to dither. In some battalions the men were instructed to count to three, or count *zwei und zwanzig, drei und zwanzig, vier und zwanzig* (22, 23, 24), before throwing so as to achieve close range detonations. This so called 'shrapnel throw' method also dealt with any enemy who had the temerity to try to snatch up and throw back German bombs. At army level this practice was strictly forbidden, however, because it was feared that slow counters would be blown to pieces or the anxious might throw hasty and wide.

Just what it was like to be caught on the receiving end of the *Handgranatentrupp* was recorded by Lieutenant Charles Carrington of the Royal Warwickshires on the Somme in 1916. First came the sound of distant voices, then a moment of terror, when the mind was full of 'Prussian Guardsmen, burly and brutal, and bursting bombs, and hand to hand struggles with cold steel'. Next came the reality, explosions filling the air with whining fragments, bay by bay, and closer with each passing second. At just such a moment Carrington risked a look over the top: 'Thirty or forty yards away I saw a hand and a grey sleeve come up out of the trench and throw a cylinder on the end of a wooden rod. It turned over and over in the air, and seemed to take hours to approach. It fell just at the foot of the traverse where we stood, and burst with a shattering shock. "The next one will get us", I thought. Sergeant Adams pulled a bomb out his pocket and threw it. I did the same and felt immediately better. A young Lance – Corporal, Houghton, did the same. The next German bomb fell short. Then someone threw without remembering to pull the pin, and in a moment the bomb was caught up and thrown

back at us by the enemy... I snapped off my revolver twice at glimpses of the enemy'.

Carrington was wounded by an egg bomb soon afterwards, and it took a bloody counter attack to drive the Germans out. Yet the feelings of trepidation were universal: from a field hospital on the other side of the line, infantryman Helmut Zschuppe recorded that 'after an attack in a trench with bombs and flamethrowers one's very soul is seared'.

Flamethrowers made their debut in early 1915, and by the end of that year the General Staff had issued detailed instructions for their use. Large static flame projectors were built into sapheads as close to the enemy line as practicable and were

Above right, NCOs pictured at Bremen. Prior to the war, the officer class was closed to men without social status and at the same time establishments allowed for fewer commissioned officers than in many armies. The result was considerable reliance upon the NCO. Senior grades of NCO such as *Feldwebel* and *Vizefeldwebel* were portepée ranks allowing the holder to carry a sword. Note also the *Schützenschnur* or marksman's lanyard, and document wallet pushed into the jacket front of the other man. *SB*

Above far right, A studio portrait of a Sergeant of *9. Rheinisches Infanterie-Regiment Nr 160,* wearing the peaked service cap or *Dienstmütze.* Peaked caps were worn by all ranks for 'walking out', whilst on active service they were the mark of the officer and NCO. The success of new small unit tactics depended much on the availability of imaginative non-commissioned officers. With the Prussian educational system spending 30 times as much in 1901 as it had done in 1870, there were now plenty of men capable of dealing with written orders, manuals, and administration. *SB*

fired just prior to the assault. The objective was to burn out or to suppress the enemy in the immediate vicinity before the attacking troops advanced. Small man pack projectors accompanied the assault of the infantry and pioneers, singling out blockhouses and machine gun nests for special attention. They could also go down the trenches adding a new and terrifying facet to the bombing attack. Where possible flame attacks were to be launched with as many projectors as available, and without any lengthy preparation by artillery: assault troops would rush in within a minute of the first flames, driving through to the enemy second or third lines.

The troops following up the flame attack were usually limited in number but commonly divided into four groups. The assault party proper, including bombers, engineers with demolition charges, and the small flamethrowers were in the vanguard. A more conventionally equipped consolidating party followed to take up and defend the ground, using loophole plates, sandbags and spades to improve the defences. Communicating and carrying parties ensured supplies and connections to the rear. Critically the flame attack itself was viewed as a hurricane assault : 'The duration of the flame attack is only one minute. The signal for it is given by a siren whistle, or at a given time, watches having been previously synchronised. The assaulting

A Stormtroop officer demonstrates the use of a concentrated charge of the type used to attack tanks and bunkers. The 1916 type loophole plate with shutter could be moved around but was at its most useful protecting a rifleman in defence.
TRH Pictures

troops must be instructed that they have nothing to fear from flames and smoke, nor need they fear that they themselves be caught by the fire jet, as this is cut off by simply turning a tap previous to their advance. They must understand they can advance immediately after the cessation of the spray without danger, as small bursts of flame on the ground or in the enemy's trenches will burn out at once, and a little fire on the ground is at once extinguished when trodden upon. It is most important to impress upon the troops that the assault is much facilitated by the use of the flame projector, as it has been proved by experience that the enemy fires very little or not at all after a flame attack.'

As special tactics developed for the use of *Nahkampfsmittel*, or weapons of close combat, there was similarly a minor revolution in machine gun tactics, though given the weapons available this took longer to come to fruition. At the beginning of the war, the issue machine gun was the MG 08, a reliable and accurate, if heavy, water cooled weapon for sustained fire. It was at its best fired from prepared positions, yet even in 1914 it was carried up close behind the assault waves in order to provide support against determined resistance. This was made slightly easier by the fact that the *Schlitten* or sledge mount could be collapsed and carried by the corners, in the manner of a stretcher, using either two or four men as porters. The gun could also be covered against observation and the elements even when on the move. Early in the war, British troops interpreted this as a deliberate ruse to impersonate a stretcher party.

This did not, however, turn the MG 08 into an assault weapon overnight, and it would see undoubtedly its most deadly work in defence. A good picture of how this was done may be gleaned from the printed 'Regulations for Machine Gun Officers and Non Commissioned Officers', and orders to Bavarian 6th Division, both of which appeared in 1916. According to these documents, machine gun emplacements were to be made as unobtrusive as possible, and usually at least two firing positions were to be provided. Only during an engagement was firing to take place from these special positions, and as a matter of principle any other daily firing which was needed was to be done from elsewhere taking pains not to damage the defensive wire entanglements.

In regular trench systems, guns were ideally provided with deep dugouts with several exits, and brought out only when the bombardment ceased. Since this took time, the MG 08 was usually positioned in the second or third line of trenches. Any extra machine guns were best kept in the rear:

'...in deep pits which are usually covered over and also on platforms concealed in trees in such a manner that the enemy is caught in an unexpected cross fire if he breaks through. The important point is that the machine guns should not, in any circumstances, be detected beforehand. They must not, therefore, be too close to the trenches which can be photographed, or to well defined woods which the enemy will suspect in any case. The best sites are in the open, in or under clumps of trees and bushes, or in hedges. All the earth extracted must be removed or concealed under hedges, etc. A low network of tripwires has proved to be the best form of obstacle. To each machine gun there should be allotted a certain number of infantrymen armed with handgrenades who can also work the gun if necessary'.

In prepared dugouts a place was provided not only for the gun but for a 'belt store of ammunition. In addition to the sixteen filled belts with the gun, the belt store was expected to have a minimum holding of 5,000 rounds plus a last ditch reserve of 2,500 rounds to be used only in a dire emergency. Any gun crew with less than this figure (a grand total of 11,500 rounds) was expected to report the fact immediately to the 'sector machine gun officer', who would approach the company commander for more.

That the MG 08 was not the best design for the offensive role was soon demonstrated by innovative Allied use of light machine weapons, most notably the American designed, but British built, Lewis gun. This was handy enough to take forward with the attack, and could be quickly deployed by one man, yet still provided enough volume of fire to make it valuable to a flexible forward defence. Whenever they could, the German troops captured them and turned them on their former owners, even going so far as to have them converted to German calibre and a manual issued for their use. Despite a limited use of various foreign and home grown automatic rifles and light machine guns, including the Danish designed Madsen, this would be a problem which was not easily solved. The result was that light 'trench mounts' were often improvised in an attempt to make the MG 08 more handy; yet even on the Somme a report submitted by German IV Corps observed that 'All regiments are unanimous in recommending the introduction of a lighter form of machine gun carriage'.

The result was the MG 08/15. For a 'light' machine gun, this was still a monster, for despite reductions in mass achieved by slimming down the receiver walls, a smaller feed block, a slimmer water jacket, and dispensing with the heavy mount in favour of a handy little bipod, the MG 08/15 still

A sentry of *8. Württembergishes Infanterie -Regiment Nr 127*, observing through a sand bag covered periscope at Hill 60, near Ypres, 1916. Grenades served as defensive as well as offensive weapons. The close combat manual left it to the discretion of the individual to choose the vital moment to change from other weapons to the bomb.
IWM Q 45395

weighed 14 kg empty. A full water jacket and magazine brought the total weight to 22 kg. Not surprisingly the MG 08/15 was widely regarded as an inferior weapon to the Lewis gun. Nevertheless the MG 08/15 did most of what was wanted, and could, if needs be, be carried and fired by one man.

By March 1917, the approved scale of issue was three guns per infantry company throughout the army, a figure which was later raised to six guns per company, or two for every platoon. At first the guns were kept in a separate fourth 'support' platoon, but eventually when numbers allowed, the light machine guns were parcelled out to the platoons, so that each platoon now had a light machine gun squad. Ultimately, in the final days of the war there were even *Einheits-Gruppe*, fully integrated squads which included a light machine gun. In the same way that the Lewis gun steadily became the bedrock of British infantry tactics, the MG 08/15 became the basic support weapon of the Germans.

It was intended to be rushed forward with the attack in order to support the riflemen or deal with strong points, and in the defence it was to add flexibility, economising on front line troops.

HOLDING THE LINE

It is interesting to observe that as the offense developed, so did the defence and as the German army spent considerable periods of time holding the line it was instrumental in the process. These new methods included not only better trenches, and the advent of ferro concrete defensive works, but larger deeper shelters to the rear, known as *Stollen*, in which reserves could be housed. Such deep constructions worked best in firm conditions, away from the bogs of Flanders. Ernst Jünger recalled that at Monchy on the Somme he had both a shallow dug out for quiet times, lit by a shaft of light, and, 'an underground dwelling approached by forty steps hewn in the solid chalk, so that even the

'The Kaiser with the fighters on the Aisne'. The group includes not only the Kaiser, but, left of centre, the Crown Prince wearing the undress cap of the *Leib-Husaren*. The Kaiser's personal standard accompanies the Imperial group. *SB*

heaviest shells at this depth made no more than a pleasant rumble when we sat there over interminable games of cards. In one wall I had a bed hewn out as immense as the box beds of Westphalian cottages, where protected from the slightest noise and encased in stout oaken boards, I slept in a casket of soft dry chalk. At its head hung an electric light... '

New constructions were but part of the story. Perhaps most importantly it was learned that a single line of trenches, thickly manned, could prove fragile in the face of overwhelming artillery followed by determined attack. The result was that as time progressed defences were laid out as deep positions within which there would be several lines, and the defenders learned eventually not to hold at all costs, but to react flexibly and expel the exhausted and battered enemy by well timed counter attack. The officer who would become most closely associated with these 'elastic' minor tactical methods was Colonel Fritz von Lossberg. Just how complex a 'deep' deployment could appear is confirmed by trench maps of the period: some German positions on vulnerable sections of the Western Front included not only apparently large empty areas, but as many as eight or nine belts of wire, and ten or more lines of trenches.

An important landmark in the evolution of the new holding tactics was the issue of a new manual on the defensive battle issued to all divisions in December 1916, which showed that the need for flexibility had been accepted and embraced at the highest level. As Ludendorff observed, decentralisation and the use of localised initiative was a risky business, but one which could pay considerable dividends: '...a new system was devised, which by distribution in depth and the adoption of a loose formation, enabled a more active defence to be maintained. It was of course intended that the position should remain in our hands at the end of the battle, but the infantryman need no longer say to himself: "here I must stand or fall, " but had, on the contrary, the right, within certain limits, to retire in any direction before strong enemy fire. Any part of the line that was lost was to be recovered by counter attack. The *Gruppe*, on the importance of which many intelligent officers had insisted before the war, now became officially the tactical unit of the infantry. The position of the NCO as leader of the *Gruppe* thus became more important. Tactics became more and more individualised.'

Greater individuality also meant that motivation was more of an issue than hitherto. As Ernst Jünger put it, 'a leader of troops today sees little of his men in the sea of smoke, and cannot compel them to be heroes'. He had to be able to rely on them, and could only do so 'if he has trained them to take the initiative rather than to act as puppets who carry out movements at the word of command'.

Eventually defensive positions would be divided into three zones: the forward outposts, the main and rear battle zones. The outposts, which mainly consisted of scattered machine gun posts or 'resistance nests' with interlocking fire zones, might well be two or more kilometres in depth, yet contained a mere ten percent of the total defenders. These *Wiederstandnester* formed a sort of net, ensnaring and holding the enemy thrust. Even if the enemy broke through, and the defenders forced to withdraw, the impetus of the attack would be slowed and blunted, caught by

Men of a *Handgranatentrupp* of *Füsilier-Regiment Fürst Karl Anton von Hohenzollern Nr 40*. The troops are festooned with stick grenades and ammunition bandoliers: several also wear improvised assault packs with greatcoat or *Zeltbahn* wrapped around a mess tin. The spikes have been removed from the *Pickelhauben* in accordance with orders of late 1915.

artillery barrages and machine gun fire from odd angles. The area thus became a patch work of *Flachen und Lucken*, 'defended areas' and swept 'gaps', into which the enemy pressed and exposed themselves to retaliation. The 'main' position was of similar depth but was located on reverse slopes where possible, and contained a greater number of men whose duty included the protection of the forward field gun lines. The most important concentrations of troops were kept back in the rear zone, which contained not only the bulk of the artillery but formations whose main purpose was the counter attack.

Though it could be regarded as both offensive and defensive, sniping also developed during 'position warfare'. It was valuable not only because it took casualties and terrorised the opposition, but because it would allow friendly troops to gather intelligence and dominate the space in front of the line. In this mysterious art the German soldier gained an early lead, aided by the fact that hunting was a well established sport at home. Thus it was that many sporting rifles with telescopic sights were rushed to the front, prior to the adoption of an issue weapon. Ideally sniper rifles were given to the best shots, and used only when a good target presented itself.

Snipers were given latitude to move away from

A field kitchen of Saxon *Jäger-Bataillon Nr 12*, in the Macedonian mountains. This unit was distinguished by the numeral '12' on its shoulder strap together with a hunting horn. The man being served is wearing the 1916 *Stahlhelm*, and on his belt has an early type cloth gas mask case, entrenching tool, steel hilted *ersatz* bay- onet and water bottle. The next man in line is wearing the distinctive Saxon type *Jäger* shako with cover. On both the Southern and Eastern fronts German sol- diers were usually regarded as more reliable than their Austrian Allies, being better equipped, and often more offensively minded.
IWM Q 29981

their parent units, into no man's land if necessary, and frequently operated as two man teams with one man observing with binoculars. Their chances were improved both by the fact that German parapets were often deliberately left untidy, which broke up the outlines of the sniper, and by the use of sacking robes which looked like sand bags. Charles Carrington gave a chilling account of what it was like to gain the attentions of enemy sharpshooters on the Somme. As his men were repairing a traverse, he recalled, 'the same sniper fired again from the village to our left, and a man called Pratt dropped like a stone just where the Corporal had fallen. He, too, had a small round hole in his temple and the back of his skull blown away. Pratt was beyond hope. His head was shattered: splatterings of brain lay in the pool of blood under him; but though he had never been conscious since the shot was fired, he refused to die. An old Corporal looked after him, held his body in his arms, which writhed and fought feebly as he lay. It was over two hours before he died...'

STORM TROOPS

On 2 March 1915, came a signal event in the history of the development of the Stormtrooper, for on that date army command entrusted VIII Corps with the formation of an ad hoc *Sturmabteilung*, literally a storm, or assault, detachment, which would come to be led by Major Kalsow of *Pionier Bataillon 18*. Rather than create an entirely new unit from scratch, personnel were seconded from *Ersatz* battalions, to make up two pioneer companies and a gun section. The prime purpose of the exercise was to test and establish a modus operandi for a new Krupp 37mm light field gun which was dubbed a *Sturmkannone*. By the end of May 1915, the 649 officers and men of *Sturmabteilung* Kalsow had established tactics by which the *Sturmkannonen* were brought up close to the enemy trenches and used in a direct fire role whilst small parties of pioneers advanced on the enemy position, which was later to be consolidated by the infantry. The experiment was not a great success, since when Kalsow's unit was eventually committed to action in small combat groups, 30 % of the men were casualties within two weeks.

The importance of these events has been disputed by academics, as it is clear that *Stoss* or shock tactics of a crude sort using grenades and other close combat weapons like trench knives and pistols were already in use irrespective of Kalsow and his task force. Yet the first official *Sturmabteilung* was significant, if only because it demonstrated that the need for new tactics was taken seriously at the highest level, and that there

was a will to set up experimental and training units for their promulgation. The precedent of integrated special purpose assault groups was firmly established, and would go on to bear considerable fruit when, after August 1915 Major Kalsow was replaced by *Hauptmann* Willy Rohr.

Hauptmann Rohr was a pre-war professional soldier and a native of Metz, first commissioned into *3. Magdeburgisches Infanterie-Regiment Nr 66*. Having undertaken various postings as adjutant and instructor, he was transferred briefly to *10. Rheinisches Infanterie-Regiment Nr 161*, before taking up a command in the prestigious *Garde Schützen* in 1913. As he soon demonstrated his mettle against the French he seemed the ideal candidate for the command of a new and innovative unit. So it was that *Sturmabteilung* Kalsow was hurriedly rechristened *Sturmabteilung* Rohr, and was soon operating with a troop of four mortars, a six machinegun platoon, and a troop of six flamethrowers in addition to its previous establishment. *Sturmabteilung* Rohr first saw action on 12 October 1915 in co-operation with *Infanterie-Regiment Nr 187* against the *Schratzmannle*. The combination of new weapons and aggressive small unit tactics proved an indisputable, if costly, success.

Early the next year, Rohr's unit was further expanded and transferred to the vital Verdun sector, becoming *Sturmbataillon* Rohr on 1 April 1916. Development and experiment, training, and actual battle action carried on apace. *Sturmbatallion* Rohr not only acted in concert with other units, but was amongst the first to wear the new steel helmets in action, received howitzers to replace the 37mm guns and support from a *Garde Pionier* flamethrower company. By May 1916, Chief of Staff Falkenhayn had taken the important decision that all armies on the Western Front would send officers and men to Rohr for training in the new methods. These disciples would then spread the training within their own formations, and certain *Jäger* battalions were selected for retraining en masse so that these too would be able to spread the new tactics.

The new 'Stormtroopers' were met with a mixture of admiration and suspicion by their less martial colleagues, as was recorded by German medical officer Stephen Westman, 'The men of the storm battalions were treated like football stars. They lived in comfortable quarters, they travelled to the 'playing ground' in buses, they did their jobs and disappeared again, and left it to the poor foot sloggers to dig in, to deal with counter attacks and to endure the avenging artillery fire of the enemy... They moved like snakes over the ground, camouflaged and making use of every bit of cover, so that they did not offer any targets for artillery fire. And when they reached the barbed wire entanglements opposite they had special torpedoes with which they blew up the defences – dangerous people to come up against.'

By the end of 1916, there would be a proliferation of *Sturmabteilungen* and *Sturmbatallione* throughout the divisions of the Western Front, and the Stormtrooper was an established fact. As Ludendorff would later explain 'Storm battalions had proved their high value both intrinsically and for the improvement of the infantry generally. They were examples to be imitated by other men.' As soon as possible the new *Sturmbatallione* would impart their combined weapons and close combat training to the army as a whole. So general would the new methods become that even *Landwehr* regiments were boasting a designated *Stosstrupp* in 1918, and by the last few months of the war some of the designated training *Sturmbatallione* were actually dispersed. By then a majority of the infantry could be thought of as 'Stormtroop' trained.

As the process was one of continual development, with frequent if minor changes of equipment and personnel, the *Sturmbataillone* often lacked a uniform establishment. Generally

Stormtroops practice the attack, Sedan, May 1917. A lightly equipped group rushes forward, carbines slung. Grenades are kept handy in bags around the neck. *IWM Q 48453*

they included a *Stab* or staff headquarters of between 40 and 70; five *Sturmkompagnien* or storm companies with four or five officers and about 250 men, and one or two machine gun companies of initially six, later 12 guns with four officers and first 85, later 135 men. The battalion *Flammenwerfertrupp* or flamethrower platoon, which remained part of the *Garde Reserve Pionier*, fielded from four to eight flamethrowers; and the *Infanterie-Geschutz-Batterie* and the *Minenwerferkompagnie* each had four guns or mortars with a complement of about 100.

SPRING OFFENSIVE 1918

In the light of the above it may legitimately be asked why the Stormtrooper became so particularly associated with the *Kaiserschlacht*, or spring offensive of 1918, and why the Stormtrooper of the last year of war has been surrounded by so much myth and misinformation. According to one commonly accepted story, for example, Stormtroop tactics were invented by General Oscar von Hutier in the East in 1917 and successfully employed in the capture of Riga. Hutier then transferred his new skills to the West resulting in the breakthroughs of the Spring Offensive.

To the soldiers of Gough's British Fifth Army on the Western Front, and to the public at large in the immediate aftermath of the war, this seemed like an eminently possible explanation for a surprise defeat which nearly led to disaster, and far more palatable than other alternatives. In fact, as we have noted, Stormtroop tactics were developed in the West, with Western Front armies having their *Sturmbatallion* in place by December 1916, and it was only from this time that similar units were established elsewhere. The *Sturmbataillon* on the Italian front did not appear until late 1917.

What was indisputably new about the German Spring Offensive of 1918 was that for the first time an attack was being undertaken in the West essentially unfettered by the war in the East.

In 1917, Russia had undergone a series of political upheavals, strikes, and economic failures culminating in the Bolshevik Revolution. Peace negotiations were not begun at Brest-Litovsk until 21 December and there was still some fighting, so the High Command was forced to leave more men in the East than Ludendorff might have liked. Nevertheless, the old 'encirclement' which had so bedevilled all German strategy from Schleiffen onward appeared to be broken. Now 33 of the best divisions were able to entrain for the Western Front. The 40 divisions remaining facing Russia were very much a holding force, including as they did a high proportion of *Landwehr*, dismounted cavalry, and other second rate troops. Amongst those left behind, facing eastward, Allied Intelligence would identify 1st Cavalry, split up on 'police duties' on the Danube, in Lithuania, and in the Ukraine. The 2nd Bavarian *Landwehr*, 3rd *Landwehr*, 7th *Landwehr*, 8th Cavalry, 11th *Landwehr*, 14th *Landwehr* and 15th *Landwehr* were similarly found to have been left in the East, and all of these and others were dismissed by Allied Intelligence as 'Fourth Class'. In some of these occupation divisions it was found that many of the men were aged 35 to 40, or more

Troops carrying an improvised stretcher in a reserve line near Soissons, June 1918. Both puttees and long marching boots are in evidence, the steel helmets are fitted with sandbag covers. The light equipment carried includes water bottles, obsolete ammunition pouches, and tin gas mask containers.
IWM Q 55014

Next page, a machine gun section advances during the battle of the Aisne, 1918. Two men carry gun barrels, others ammunition belt boxes. All are lightly equipped with only gas masks, water bottles, bread bags, bayonets and entrenching tools in evidence.
IWM Q 55349

than ten years older than the average in the best combat formations.

By contrast with the situation in the East, Ludendorff graded his troops in the West so that the best trained, most active, would fall upon the Allied line and tear holes in it. Of these 44 were designated 'Mobile' divisions, with full strength 850 man battalions and the lion's share of flamethrowers, trench mortars, and machine guns. Another 30 'attack' divisions constituted the first line reserve. The remaining 100 divisions were the *Stellungs* or 'trench' divisions, presumed capable of holding the line but not up to the standard of all out assault. Extra training courses were put on, principally at Sedan and Valanciennes, to train cohorts of 80 men at a time in the latest skills including joint operations, machine gun tactics, and anti-tank work.

Significantly, the guide for much of this activity would be a new manual penned by the operations section of the General Staff entitled *Der Angriff* in *Stellungskrieg*, (*The Attack in Position Warfare*). Its contents, individually, may not have said very much which was new, but taken as a whole and applied to a major offensive it became more than the sum of its parts. Specifically, *The Attack in Position Warfare* sought to combine the best of the old with the new; encouraging 'that spirit of bold attack and will to conquer' which had characterised 1914 with the new tactics, assaults led by 'Storm Detachments', and attacking waves which could be either skirmish lines, or more assault detachments, or a combination of both, as dictated by the objective. Machine guns were to co-operate as closely as possible, being allotted to individual groups of infantry even in the first wave. Attacking infantry were to be trained against realistic objectives in practice, and when the real assault came, be prepared to 'advance into their own artillery and trench mortar fire', as was already taught in the *Sturmbatallione*. The lead assault troops were, as General Hoffman explained it, to 'test' parts of the enemy line finding the weakest areas against which to exert their force. This advanced guard would find and exploit fault lines assisted by the artillery which would fire whirlwind barrages, designed to neutralise rather than systematically pound the opposition. Once the front line had been penetrated and infiltrated the main force would be thrown in, opening up and exploiting the gaps.

Typical was the experience recorded by Leutnant Hermann Pürkhauer of the Bavarian *Infanterie-Regiment-Kronprinz*, 1st Bavarian Division. This unit undertook initial training at Machault during January 1918, followed by a three week course with Hutier's Eighteenth Army at Vervins. Remarkably for this time the troops were properly fed, and the syllabuses included not only fire training but advances in co-operation with machine guns, tanks, and divisional level attacks. On 16 March 1918, the 1st Bavarian Division began its move to the jumping off point by silent night marches. Close to the front, marching songs were forbidden and horses' hooves and wheels were deadened with sacking and straw. All unit identifiers were removed and the men issued with all forms of munitions and iron rations.

Stormtroops take advantage of the rare opportunity to use tank support, in this case a captured British Mark IV. Note the ring shaped *Wix Modell* 1917 flamethrower. Germany experimented with fortress flamethrowers in the first few years of the century, and a practical 'portable apparatus' had been patented by Richard Fiedler in 1910.
IWM Q 45348

The supporting bombardment was not to be a drawn out affair, nor were the guns engaged to be prematurely exposed to counter battery fire. To this end, battery positions were identified in advance, and shells dumped covertly and concealed. The total number of pieces gathered would be 6,473, just over half the total German artillery strength on the Western Front. More than 2,000 of them were 15 cm calibre heavies, and over 70 super heavies of 21 cm and over. The gun lines themselves were marked out in advance, as a curious Leutnant Kurt Fischer of Regiment Nr 464 observed; 'with small yellow wooden stakes stuck in the ground... hundreds of them, under every bush and in the open. Two stood in line for the wheels of a gun, a bigger post behind for the trail.' The cannonade would be brief, enough to shake up the enemy and suppress their guns, not enough for major reorganisation of their reserves. Even so, more than a million shells would be thrown at the British lines in five hours.

In some places, new positions, often disguised as shell craters, were dug just in front of the existing German trenches to house the assault companies. British guns, preregistered to hit the main line, would therefore usually miss the fresh troops until it was too late. Even so there were nightmare occasions when the assault troops lost their way or were caught by shelling, as Hauptmann Ernst Jünger of Hannoverian *Fusilier Regiment Prinz Albrecht von Preußen Nr 73* would find out : 'Sections piled arms and crowded into a gigantic crater, whilst Leutnant Sprenger and I sat on the edge of a smaller one. There had been shells falling about 100 metres in front of us for some while. Then there was one nearer; the splinters struck the sides of the hole. One of the men cried out and said that he was hit in the foot. I shouted to the men to scatter among the surrounding shell holes, and meanwhile I examined the man's boot to see if there was a hole. Then the whistle of another shell high in the air. Everyone had that clutching feeling,

"It's coming over !" There was a terrific stupefying crash. The shell had burst in the midst of us.

'I picked myself up, half unconscious. The machine gun ammunition in the large shell hole, set alight by the explosion, was burning with an intense pink glow. It illuminated the rising fumes of the shell burst, in which there writhed a heap of black bodies and the shadowy forms of survivors who were rushing from the scene in all directions. At the same time rose a multitudinous tumult of pain and cries for help. I will make no secret of it that, after a moment's blank horror, I took to my heels like the rest...'

The assault was launched on 21 March in the direction of Jussy and the Crozat Canal under cover of fog, smoke and gas, behind a creeping barrage fired by Bruchmüller's artillery. The initial gain was an unprecedented three miles, and a good bag of British prisoners, though even this was far less than planned. German casualties for this day would total 78,000: a figure claimed to be the highest tally for the whole war. March and April would claim half a million German soldiers killed, wounded and missing. Yet they kept going whenever and wherever opportunity would allow, on occasion outreaching sustainable objectives. This, however, was not the result of local enthusiasm, nor even merely the effect of of being suddenly engorged with British supplies and French wine, but a calculated gamble, and the fine level of judgment built in to *The Attack in Position Warfare*, which stated, 'In the élan of an attack, good troops often overrun the objective. A quick grasp of the situation often secures successes which otherwise could only be won by renewed preparation. Troops pressing forward therefore should not be kept too much in hand. In a breakthrough on a large scale, particularly the boldest decision is always the best. On the other hand, reverses are easily occasioned by merely rushing on without consideration...'

Nevertheless, reserves were to be committed where there were signs of success and as Private

Fred Noakes of the Coldstream Guards would relate, the effects could be dramatic: 'From where we were, we could see the Germans swarming over the ridge opposite, and pouring towards us in an endless torrent. There seemed to be thousands of them, and in their grey uniforms they looked like an army of ants. They were not in their old "mass" formation, but in "open order", which is so much more difficult to stop by artillery fire. Everyone could now see that retreat was inevitable.'

The truth was that the German Spring Offensive threw more men, better trained, and better armed, at the Allied line than ever before. Though even then the numerical advantage was marginal except in the specific sectors earmarked for the offensive. Equally the British and the French had problems of their own: the French had suffered mutinies in 1917, the British had agreed to take up more of the line, but had not committed the men to cover the space. Whilst the Germans had grown used to defensive fighting and the use of deep positions over a period of many months, the British had put most of their efforts, not into building fortifications, nor the practice of defensive warfare, but into costly offensives of very limited gain such as the Third Ypres. Though the USA had declared war on Germany in April 1917 there was as yet not much evidence on the ground of her huge potential strength, and the German General Staff was looking at its last serious window of opportunity. In short, March 1918 was a disaster waiting to happen, and the Stormtroops were just reaching their peak of efficiency. They were not new, nor had Hutier invented them personally, but he, amongst others, was ready and willing to use them with supreme aggression. The last few months of the war would provide dramatic evidence not only of the growing numerical and logistic superiority of the Allies, but of the fact that they too had learned their own versions of Stormtroop tactics. The Spring Offensive was thus a tactical but not a strategic victory.

The tactical changes between 1914 and 1918 have rightly been described as 'epoch making', and in the German example the difference was stark. At the outbreak of war infantry had fought as companies and battalions in columns and skirmish lines armed only with rifles, machine gun companies were a support element. By 1918, Stormtroop tactics had evolved to the extent that a squad of ten or twelve could include the full gamut of infantry weapons, and units as small as a light machine gun *Trupp* of just four men could be accounted of tactical value.

DEVELOPMENT OF UNIFORM

When the German infantryman went to war in 1914, he was essentially a rifleman clad in the field grey service version of the blue uniforms in which his predecessors had defeated the Danes, Austrians, and French in the nineteenth century. His equipment consisted of a traditional backpack and ammunition pouches, and his headgear was the latest version of the *Pickelhaube* or spiked leather helmet which had first been introduced in 1842. The 1910 Model *Felduniform* was made of

Top, the shape of things to come: a soldier of the mechanical transport troops, or Kraftfahrtruppen, which provided drivers for trucks and tanks, pictured at Wiesbaden. Shortages of materials as well as the priority given to artillery and machine guns meant that mechanised warfare would remain relatively undeveloped in Germany during the Great War. **SB**

Above, a typical selection of uniform c. 1916. Amongst the officers in the front row can be seen three types of jacket; the undress double breasted *Litewka* with its distinctive collar patches; the single breasted 1910 model *Feldrock* ; and second from right the *Bluse* with its fly front. All officers have rank boards at the shoulder, and two collar *Litzen*. **TRH Pictures**

wool and consisted of a traditionally styled jacket (the *Waffenrock* or *Feldrock*) and trousers; in field grey for the majority of the army and grey green for the *Jäger*. The eight buttoned jacket with stand and fall collar had many distinctions which were carried over from the old *Dunkleblau* which had so recently been abandoned by the regulars, and which was retained by some of the *Landwehr* and *Landsturm*, even in 1914. These distinctions were primarily in the shoulder straps, pipings, cuff details, buttons, and collar bars or *Litzen*.

The shoulder straps of the infantry were marked with the regimental number in red, or with cyphers of monarchs or other patrons for many of the senior regiments. The piping of the shoulder strap denoted regimental seniority in Guards regiments, and army corps in the case of the line. Corps I, II, IX, X, XII, and I Bavarian all had a white shoulder strap piping; III, IV, XI, XIII, XV, XIX and II Bavarian had red; V, VI, XVI, XVII, and III Bavarian had yellow; VII, VIII, XVIII, and XX had light blue; and XXI had light green. Collars, jacket front edge, and rear skirt ornaments were also piped; scarlet for infantry and machine gunners; green for *Jäger*; and green with black collar piping for the *Schützen*. Cuffs were usually of the Brandenburg style with a vertical flap and three buttons; but the cuffs of the *Jäger*, *Garde zu Fuß* and certain of the grenadier regiments, were of the Swedish type having two horizontal buttons. Buttons were of a state design, usually bearing a crown motif, though those of the Bavarians had a lion. The *Litzen* appeared as a single or double bar of decoration on the collar and on the cuff buttons, and at this period were limited to certain senior regiments such as the guards and grenadiers.

Similar distinctions denoting both troop type and state of origin were carried on the headgear. The leather *Pickelhaube*, and the shako of the Jägers and machine gunners had a state helmet plate, which in the case of guards units also incorporated a star motif. Both the helmet and the soft peakless cap or *Feldmütze* also carried cockades, one for the

Empire the other for the state. The Imperial or Reichs cockade was red white and black; the Prussian black and white; the Bavarian white and light blue; the Saxon green and white.

Unsurprisingly, the demands of war, reorganisations, and an expansion of the army to six million men made it impossible to keep up either the quality of materials, or the mass of fussy details which had been the pride of the German army. First to go were the shoulder strap pipings, cuff and skirt details on the jackets, resulting in what later became known as the Model 1914 or simplified jacket. New wool also began to run short, resulting in the use of recycled cloth and experiment with substitute fibres. At the same time, leather supply was reduced and *Pickelhauben* began to be made from felt, tin, and other materials, producing the so called *Ersatz Pickelhaube*.

In 1915 it was recognised that a radical change was required, and so on 21 September an Imperial cabinet order was issued which announced a new uniform which swept away much of the detail, and economised on scarce materials. The jacket of the new ensemble, known as the *Bluse* was based on

Below, shoulder strap cyphers of the infantry. The devices were worked in red on a field grey backing. In 1914, the straps were piped in the corps colours, but from 1915 infantry straps were either piped white, or the piping was omitted entirely. *From Handbook of the German Army 1918*

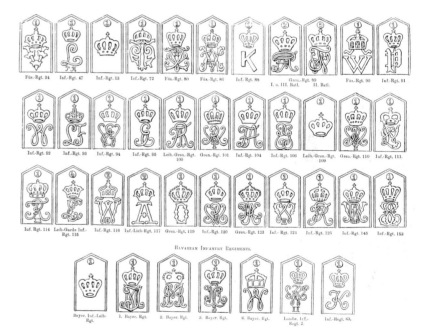

the old undress *Litewka*. It was fly fronted, lacked the pipings, had only small *Litzen* where appropriate, and was not worn with bandsmens' wings or other frippery. Shoulder straps were rationalised so that pipings now represented troop types rather than formations; regimental numbers or cyphers also continued to be worn. Belts, boots and other leatherwork were now to be produced in black, though state belt plates were retained. Ankle boots and puttees, which had originally been a distinction of *Jäger* and other specialists were now allowed to the infantry. Leather patches appeared on trousers and were commonly associated with assault troops. Though state

buttons and blue and grey Bavarian collar lace were allowed as minor distinctions, and some troops never received the new uniform, the result was to blend the whole of the Imperial German army into one amorphous mass. They all became, as one account put it, 'workers of war', in grey uniform, grey helmets, trudging through grey mud.

The ultimate expression of this totalisation of the war was perhaps the adoption of a universal, and highly effective, steel helmet, or *Stahlhelm*. Designed in 1915 as a defence against the small low velocity fragments of shells and grenades which caused the majority of head wounds, it was issued to assault troops in 1916, and thus became

Above, British Tommies wearing a selection of captured headgear. Particularly noticeable are the *Garde Kürassiere* helmet with massive eagle crest; various *Pickelhauben*, with and without parade plumes, and a *Leib* hussar busby with death's head plate. Such finery was swept away with the introduction of the steel helmet. Cavalry ceased to be effective in the assault, and if not dismounted was relegated to scouting and police duties mainly on the Eastern Front. **SB**

Right, the new small unit tactics and the 'empty battlefield': carefully camouflaged troops on patrol, c.1918. **SB**

known as the Modell 1916. The distinctive shape of the German steel helmet came from the necessity to protect as much of the head as possible, whilst avoiding the back pack, and obscuring the sights of the rifle when shooting. It was also consciously influenced by mediaeval designs. An innovative three pad liner system improved fit and reduced the shock of blows to the helmet shell. The strange lugs projecting on either side, present on both the model 1916, and slightly modified model 1918 steel helmets were intended to support an optional thick frontal plate. The lugs were hollow down the centre, and thus doubled as vents.

Contrary to popular belief there was relatively little to distinguish Stormtroops from other soldiers, particularly later on in the war when huge numbers were storm troop trained. Though assault troops were often the first to receive steel helmets, puttees, and ankle boots, these were all generally worn in 1918, and similarly early uniform features were occasionally retained by men within assault units. This lack of clear cut distinction was partly because men from throughout the army were drawn upon to create the *Sturmkompagnien* and *Sturmbatallione*, and because old uniform and footwear was kept until worn out.

Regulations of February and March 1917 stated that all personnel of *Sturmkompagnien* and machine gun units were to wear infantry uniform, whilst mortar companies wore Pionier uniform and infantry gun battery crews dressed as artillery. Men of the *Sturmbatallione* were clothed as infantry, and were to have the number of their battalion in red on their shoulder strap, mortar crews wore a red 'MW' and numeral on a black shoulder strap. Flamethrower troops were granted a death's head badge for the sleeve in July 1916. The only exceptions to these general rules were Rohr's *Sturmbatallion Nr 5*, which wore Pionier uniform and *Jäger-Sturmbatallion Nr 3* which retained *Jäger* uniform. Some temporary distinctions were also used, including white brassards or white patches on the

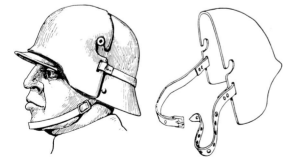

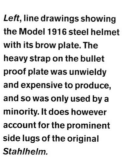

Left, line drawings showing the Model 1916 steel helmet with its brow plate. The heavy strap on the bullet proof plate was unwieldy and expensive to produce, and so was only used by a minority. It does however account for the prominent side lugs of the original **Stahlhelm**.

Top, the 1916 model **Stahlhelm**. The disruptive 'lozenge' camouflage pattern is of the type in use in 1918, with angular patches of green, rust brown, and yellow ochre divided by black lines. *SB*

Above, interior of the 1916 steel helmet showing the liner with three leather covered pads and the manner in which the chin strap is secured to the helmet shell. *SB*

back which were used by night raiding parties. These were discontinued, however, as they not only helped to identify friendly troops but tended to give away raiders to the enemy. According to certain accounts, arm bands with a letter 'S' were occasionally worn by some assault troops.

PERSONAL EQUIPMENT

The basic infantry equipment of 1914 was closely based on nineteenth century antecedents. Vital to the wearing of pretty well all the equipment was the field belt or *Feldkoppel*, which was of leather with state motif buckle, and was supported in place by belt hooks which were integral to the uniform jacket. The belt equipment usually comprised the bayonet in its leather frog, with or without a decorative coloured woollen company knot; ammunition pouches; water bottle and bread bag. An entrenching tool or a hatchet in a leather carrier, knife, or other items were added as required. A cloth gas mask case was introduced in 1915, but from 1916 this was progressively superseded by a small tin cylinder. Many troops, especially in the *Landwehr*, had worn beards in 1914, but these steadily disappeared amongst front line troops later in the war as a close fitting mask became regarded as a necessity.

The standard infantry ammunition pouch was the leather 1909 model *Patronentasche* which was divided into three sections. Each pouch carried 60 rounds, so the pair of pouches totalled 120 cartridges. Metal loops allowed the pack straps to be attached. Not all troops received the new 1909 pouches, and so obsolete types remained in use, particularly with the *Landwehr* and *Landsturm*. The commonest of these was the 1895 model pouch, a rectangular leather box with a 45 round capacity. The bread bag or *Brotbeutel* was a small haversack to hold rations, metal mug, and extra ammunition. It was fabricated of reddish brown or field grey canvas, and if not suspended from the belt could be carried over the shoulder by means of

a strap. The one litre felt or fabric covered *Feldflasche* was carried by most personnel; medics were often supplied with a two litre flask.

Food came in two major forms: communally cooked and served rations; and the iron ration which each man carried to be consumed when cooked meals could not reach him from the company field kitchen. Either way what was eaten bore steadily less resemblance to what would be regarded as edible or desirable in peace time. As the enemy blockade reduced imports, and the German people ate their way through the produce of home and occupied lands, unappealing *Ersatz* or substitute foods bulked ever larger in the dwindling larder. Acorn coffee and bread padded out with every form of grain are well known, but a bewildering variety of things of dubious nutritional value found their way to the front. As officer Ernst Jünger recalled when in France, 'Schüddekopf wakes me at about five on his return from Puisieux, to whose outskirts the cooker brings coffee, water, 'portions' [rations], and the letters every morning. I jump up and go straight out into the trench. My helmet is filled with water, a tumbler and my washing apparatus are already set out on a ledge. After washing I sit down on the bench and drink my coffee at leisure. Unfortunately there is little to be said for it. Nor is the portion very bewitching. Lately we have been given a paste of ground flesh fibre to eat with our bread. All the same it is a slight improvement on the yellow fat, monkey fat we used to call it, that we had previously – extracted, as I have heard, from the heads of herrings. One has in any case to be very cautious with it ; for the huge glistening flies in their buzzing multitudes are crazy to seize any opportunity to deposit their packet of eggs in it'. Dead horses which had often been left where they fell in 1914, or covered with quick lime, became a delicacy by 1918. First great steaks would disappear from their hams and shoulders; then smaller pieces would find their way into the stew pots and dixies.

Infantry equipment: the grey canvas Zeltbahn, mess tin and water bottle.
King's Liverpool Regiment

The infantry back pack was the framed *Tornister 95 für Fusstruppen* with leather shoulder straps and a flapped closure. Originally covered in panels of natural cow hide which retained the hair, it was soon simplified and the cow hide gradually substituted with red brown, or more commonly, grey, canvas. At the start of the war *Jäger* had a distinctive black leather pack, with badger skin flap, though this was seldom seen later. The *Tornister* had compartments for clothing, food, cartridges, and a bag for tent accessories. On the march the tent section, or *Zeltbahn*, and the greatcoat could be secured around the pack by means of leather straps, and the mess tin or *Kochgeshirr* could be attached to the flap of the pack. In the field personal eating utensils usually took the form of a folding fork and spoon: trench knives and bayonets could be used for cutting and carving.

Due to its appearance, the hairy back pack was sometimes referred to as the 'monkey', and very often it was crammed with less than regulation equipment. Student Martin Müller, for example, recorded how he readied himself during an alarm at Christmas 1914, 'Besides underclothing, knitted helmet, and the other things which went into one's pack, I crammed in a sausage, some ginger bread, the marzipan and all the fags. All the rest, – blankets, pillow, cape, jam, boxes, the little

Christmas tree, and all sorts of other things – I chucked anyhow into my kit bag. I hastily buckled my Kodak onto my belt and – still with a great piece of cake in one hand – stuck Herr Grossman's bottle of concentrated tea and rum [*Jägertee*] into my bread sack, seized 'the pop gun', and rushed out!

Even without extra loot and festive goodies, the full marching equipment with camping gear and spare clothes weighed a total of about 55 lb. That this was far too much for the attack was readily understood. Thus it was that even from the beginning of the war a 'fighting order' was frequently adopted without the clumsy pack, and very often the great coat or tent section was tied around the shoulder. Soon other improvisations were in use: *Sturmgepäck* or assault packs might consist of the *Zeltbahn* tied around the mess tin, or a great coat and *Zeltbahn* folded into a rough oblong and tied on the back with straps. Extras such as empty sand bags, spades, portable saws, wire cutters and grenade bags could be added as required. Helmut Strassmann, fighting on the Eastern Front in the summer of 1915, recorded how for the attack inessentials were reduced and firepower increased. In his case this meant carrying a load comprising 'wire cutter, five bombs, two iron rations and 200 cartridges'. The assault order as specified for a soldier advancing in the wake of

Interior of a 1915 dated grey canvas back pack or *Tornister*, marked to the Prussian Guard. Though the old natural cowhide panels have been deleted the traditional layout is retained with separate compartments for clothing and rations and two small pockets or *Patronenbehälter* in the corners of the flap accommodating a total of 30 cartridges. The long bag, fastened with two buttons, is the *Zeltzubehörbeutel* or case for tent poles and pegs. **SB, MS**

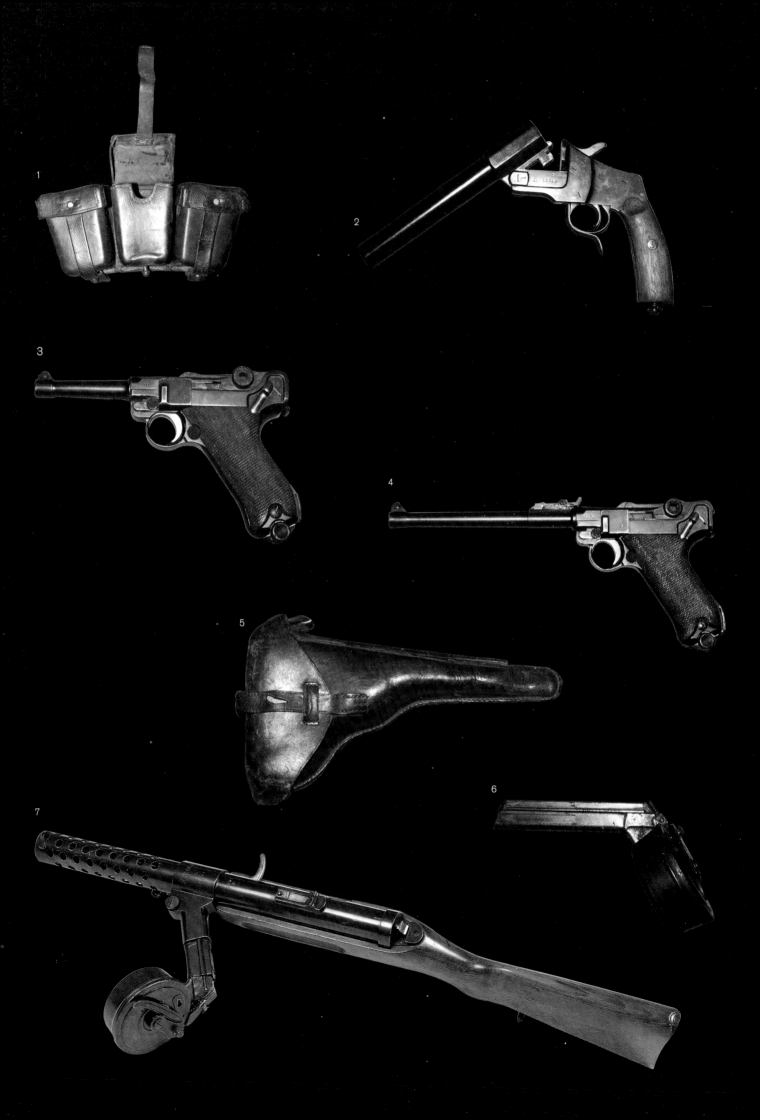

flame attacks at the end of 1915 comprised 'greatcoat, *Zeltbahn*, mess tin, full water bottle, four days rations in his haversack, and in addition, at least 200 rounds, two hand grenades and rifle with fixed bayonet'.

There was a degree of artistry involved in making up an assault pack, and to produce a handy kit took practice. In one method of preparation, Walter Beumelburg described how the assault pack was begun with a mess tin, around which were the coat and blanket, secured with the bread bag strap. Finishing touches included a canvas breech cover for the rifle, and two field dressings sewn inside the front of the jacket. Officer Ernst Jünger had his batman prepare his battle pack for him. This was essentially a haversack into which went bread, jam, mug, pipe, tobacco, toothbrush and notebook, whilst an outside pocket contained four egg bombs and a metal flask. Also carried were his pistol, map case and water bottle.

FIREPOWER

The main issue rifle of the infantry at the outbreak of war was the *Gewehr* 98 Mauser, a five shot bolt action model which was accurate to long range, fairly soldier proof, and had an overall length of 125 cm. This length was calculated for well aimed shots, and provided reach in a bayonet fight, yet was less than handy in the confined space of a trench or when carried over rough ground at the double. From the start there were insufficient rifles to go round with the result that many second line formations, including much of the *Landwehr* and *Landsturm*, was armed with obsolete weapons, primarily the Mauser G 88, of which about half a million were still on hand in 1914. With rapid victories over the Russians, a mass of Moisin Nagant rifles fell into German hands and these helped to obviate shortages. Another method adopted to increase the supply of arms was the use of a wide variety of subcontractors to make parts for the G98. The result was that the rifles made up from these varied supplies did not necessarily have fully interchangeable parts, and were accordingly marked with stars above the chamber to warn armourers of this fact.

Whilst well designed for a medium to long range fire fight using aimed shots it soon became obvious that the G98 and its various substitutes were not ideal for all the tasks that were demanded of the infantry by modern tactics. The result was that specialist arms were soon being introduced. The cavalry had had carbine length weapons for many years, the most recent models of which were the *Karabiner 98 A*, and the *Karabiner 98 AZ*, and in 1914 the cyclists, sharpshooters, and foot

artillery were all equipped with the AZ model. Thereafter carbines began to achieve popularity in the hands of assault formations, though total production of these was never more than about a fifth of the full length rifle.

As there were no specialist sniper weapons in 1914, the issue arms were supplemented by private purchase and commandeered sporting rifles. By 1915, however, telescopes were being officially fitted to specially selected and slightly modified G98 rifles at the factory, creating the *Scharfschützen Gewehr 98*. Used by two man teams, comprising a sniper and an observer, often from behind steel loop hole plates, the sniper rifle could be a useful weapon to terrorise or pick off the opposition. Particularly tempting targets were provided by enemy officers, as was recorded by Lieutenant Cloete of the King's Own Yorkshire Light Infantry, 'That was what the Germans did to us and they had no difficulty as we wore officers' uniforms with long tunics, riding breeches, trench boots and Sam Browne belts. This was one reason the officers' casualties were so high.' The Germans had a further advantage in their sniping. With them it was done by their *Jäger* battalions, picked sharpshooters who in peacetime had been game keepers and guides. They wore green uniforms instead of grey and were permanently stationed in one sector, so they knew every blade of grass in front of them and spotted the slightest change.' The *Jäger* may have been the best, but sniper skills were soon being developed widely throughout the army.

Length and suitability for sniping were only part of the rifle problem since the conditions of trench warfare and close assault brought with them distinct tactical problems which simply had not existed in open warfare. It was now almost always the case that the enemy remained totally out of sight for long periods, which were punctuated by moments of frenetic activity during which a trench was stormed. At which times there were either fleeting glimpses of the opposition, or a sudden profusion of close range targets. A five round bolt action rifle was simply not the weapon for such tasks. A solution was sought with the introduction of a special large magazine for the G98, but this never became a standard issue, nor did it improve manageability.

The semi automatic pistol in the shape of the elegant Luger designed 9mm *Pistole 08* was a partial answer to the problem, for it was handy, able to deliver eight rounds rapidly, and was reloaded with a fresh magazine in about five seconds. The *Lange Pistole* version of the Luger could be fitted with a simple shoulder stock, and even with a drum

Opposite
1) The 1909 Model ammunition pouch, with its three flap topped compartments. This example in brown leather was made at Ülm in 1910. *SB*
2) The standard issue single shot signal pistol of the Great War: vital for the infantry at a time when communications were limited.
3) The 9mm, Model 1908, 'Luger' Parabellum. Inspired by an innovative, if ungainly, pistol created by Hugo Borchardt, this elegant eight round semi-automatic was perfected by Georg Luger. By 1914, it was the main issue pistol of the German army, and would remain so until overtaken by the Walther P38 during the Second World War.
4, 5 & 6) The Luger Lange Pistole, also showing the 32 round drum magazine and leather holster. Though of limited effectiveness, this semi-automatic helped to demonstrate the usefulness of a repeater more compact than a rifle, yet with a higher rate of fire. The problems of close range combat would later be more effectively solved by the sub-machine gun and assault rifle.
7) The 9mm Bergmann MP18 with drum magazine; the influential German sub-machine gun design of 1917. *MOD Pattern Room/ TRH Pictures*

magazine, thereby modestly increasing range and sustained fire capacity. Yet even this was not enough, and the Luger could be prone to malfunction in dirty conditions. Moreover production of the P08 was insufficient for demand, with the result that other semi automatics like the Mauser C96 'Broomhandle', and revolvers such as the old *Reichs* model were pressed into service.

With the introduction of the Bergmann *Maschinenpistole 18*, the short range personal firepower of the Stormtrooper took a quantum leap. This revolutionary weapon, designed by Hugo Schmeisser, and accepted at the end of 1917 was the first practical, portable, sub-machine gun. It was equipped with the same 32 round snail drum which had been used with the Luger *Lange Pistole*, and was capable of emptying it in a hail of 9 mm rounds in about six seconds. It became known as the *Kugelspritz*, or 'bullet squirter'. It was planned that about ten percent of the infantry, and many officers and NCOs would be armed with the new gun; and that special machine pistol detachments would be formed within each company. Though the invention of the SMG would have a dramatic impact in the future, only about 30,000 MP 18 machine pistols were made before the end of the war.

Grenades, which had been essentially siege weapons and were the province of the Pioneer prior to the war soon assumed a much greater importance in the trenches. Initially, the main hand held models were the *Kügel* or ball hand grenade which was fitted with a time pull fuse, and the *Diskus* grenade which was shaped like an oyster and exploded on impact. These were supplemented by the rodded rifle grenades models 1913 and 1914, which had much greater range but were not terribly accurate unless used in conjunction with a launching stand. The famous stick, or *Stielhandgranate*, made its appearance in 1915, and was an offensive weapon par excellence. It would soon be regarded as the trade mark of the shock troops to the extent that a grenade-shaped badge was sometimes worn to distinguish them. The basic model of *Stielhandgranate* was the 'B.Z.', which had a cylindrical metal container for the explosive and a wooden handle. A cord passed through the handle, and emerged at the base. A smart tug on the cord lit the fuse which burned for five and a half seconds before it reached the detonator and the grenade exploded.

Grenades could also be used for close range defence in conjunction with rifle fire, as was recorded by Gustav Ebelshauser fighting with Bavarian infantry regiment Nr 17 in October 1916,

Eier or 'egg' hand grenades. A clever yet simple addition to the trench arsenal, since these small bombs could be carried in quantity and thrown further than other types. The top one was for training; the central example is fused ready for use; the other appears as it would in transit, fitted with a safety plug. *M. Seed*

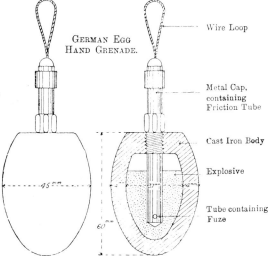

Diagram of the *Eierhand-granate*, c 1916.

The 1913 model ball hand grenade.

'Even while raising their hands in surrender the gesture was misunderstood. Bullets brought down their supplicating arms. The English might have called for mercy, but Stuermer and his men spoke another language. For their own salvation the English had to be killed. In the space of a second, Ebelshauser hesitated. A Tommy not much older than himself was staring at him. "Have pity", his gleaming, wide open eyes seemed to say. Before he could hold back, Ebelshauser's hand had mechanically thrown a grenade. In the midst of the explosion the man's eyes remained fixed on him. Ebelshauser felt relieved when he saw the Englishman drop at last. He could forget himself again and go on with the butchery. Kuefer, Glindemeyer and Schultz aimed at their own targets made of almost motionless human bodies... To their right Stuermer was conducting the throwing of hand grenades. His forehead dripped with perspiration as he picked up and passed the missiles after tearing out the fuses. All they had to do was hurl the bombs in the right direction as fast as they could.'

In 1916, egg or *Eier* bombs were introduced. These little grenades were deemed sufficient to clear a single bay within a trench system, and had the advantage that they could be carried in large numbers and thrown a long way. Rodded rifle grenades which required the use of a blank cartridge and could be vulnerable to rough handling were progressively abandoned in the middle period of the war, being effectively superseded by *Granatenwerfer* bomb throwers which were capable of launching a larger finned bomb to a range of about 300 metres. Nevertheless a new rifle grenade was introduced in 1917. This *Wurf* grenade was shaped like a small jam pot and was fired using a small discharger which fitted to the muzzle of the rifle. Unlike the rodded bombs it was launched using a normal bulleted round.

Grenades of any description were the cause of frightful wounds, and evidence of bombing would litter every field where close range fighting had taken place. As Ernst Jünger observed, 'Everywhere among the shell holes are to be seen the shallower charred depressions where bombs exploded in the stampede of hand to hand fighting. The effect of the bursts, which at this range can fling a man in the air to come down like a sack, can be seen from the dead bodies lying all about beside and over one another just as death cast them down. Their faces and bodies are riddled by splinters and their uniforms burnt and blackened by the flame of the explosive. The faces of those that lie on their backs are distorted, and their eyes wide open as though fixed upon a disaster...'

Like the grenade and pistol, bayonets, knives, trench clubs and even entrenching tools, were staples of close combat. Pre-war training had assumed that the bayonet fight would be the most usual form of close action, and to this end the issue sidearms were different forms of knife bayonet with a premium on length. Perhaps the commonest was the *Seitengewehr 98/05* a wicked looking wide bladed arm which would later be christened the 'butcher' bayonet, but there were others in use including the *Seitengewehr 98* which had an especially lengthy 52 cm blade. Though sometimes useful, knife bayonets were often too long for

Right above, the battle of Arras, April 1917, and German machine gunners emerge to be taken into captivity carrying their MG 08 stretcherwise on its sledge mount. The NCO at the fore end of the gun has 'Swedish' cuffs to his uniform, typical of machine gun units.
IWM Q 5723

Right below, the parts of the MG 08 / 15 light machine gun.

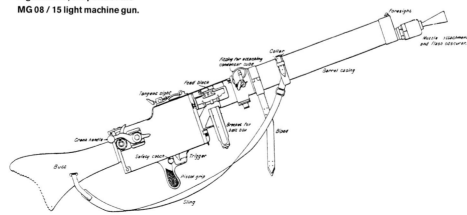

raiding or fighting within the confines of a trench, and so short bladed trench knives were soon in vogue. Trench knives, or *Nahkampfmesser*, were commonly added to the belt equipment, but some men put them down the boot, or even had a sheath stitched into their breeches. Trench clubs could also be silent pacifiers, and the majority were wooden batons between 30 and 50 cm in length. Added refinements included studs and lead weighting.

The standard machine gun at the outbreak of war was the MG 08. This was fed by 250 round belts, and water cooled, with a mechanism based on the Maxim toggle lock system. The mounting was a *Schlitten* or sledge, of adjustable height, with a

small box for tools, and provision to take an armoured shield and barrel jacket. It was capable of a cyclic rate up to 500 rounds per minute, and was excellent for creating beaten zones of sustained fire out to ranges of a mile or more. Under the right circumstances the MG 08 could be extremely effective. As was reported by an officer of *Infanterie-Regiment Nr 180* on the Somme on 1 July 1916, 'Our men at once clambered up the steep shafts leading from the dugouts to daylight and ran singly or in groups to the nearest shell craters. The machine guns were pulled out of the dugouts and hurriedly placed in position, their crews dragging the heavy

Maschinengewehr-Abteilung an der Westfront mit erbeuteten russischen Maschinengewehr.

One of many captured weapons pressed into service, the Russian Model 1905 Maxim machine gun, complete with carriage, water can and armoured shield. *SB*

ammunition boxes up the steps and out to the guns. A rough firing line was thus rapidly established... A few minutes later when the leading British line was within a hundred metres, the rattle of machine gun and rifle fire broke out along the whole line... Whole sections seemed to fall, and the rear formations, moving in close order, quickly scattered. The advance rapidly crumbled.'

Seen from the opposite side of the line the hail of fire was simultaneously dreadful and impressive, 'It was the fire of the German machine guns which was most trying to our men... A young officer of the Northumberland Fusiliers paid high tribute to them. "They are wonderful men", he said, "and work with their machines until they are bombed to death. In the trenches of Fricourt they stayed on when all other men had either been killed or wounded, and would neither surrender nor escape". '

In trench defence, it became usual to provide the MG 08 with at least two firing positions so that it could cover different fields of fire, and operate unpredictably in the face of enemy infantry and artillery. According to instructions in force during the middle period of the war each gun was kept provided with at least 11,500 rounds, and the crew were to keep hand grenades, pistols, and flare guns to hand in the event of enemy close assault.

Despite the excellence of the MG 08 as a position weapon, the major drawback was weight, for the barrel section alone weighed over 26 kg, and the *Schlitten* more than 30 kg without any armour. It was therefore difficult to move the machine gun forward fast enough to keep up with assaulting infantry, or to move the weapon rapidly within the defensive position even though this was what was intended. Many light 'trench mounts' were therefore improvised, which, though less stable and less suitable for long range fire than the sledge, were more manoeuvrable. In the face of Allied light machine guns such as the Lewis, German troops were soon demanding similar weapons of their own. Danish designed

Madsen guns were therefore issued in small numbers from 1915 for *Musketen* battalions, and captured light machine guns were turned on their former owners; but this was nothing like a complete answer.

For this reason the MG 08 / 15 was introduced. It was no great technological departure, being very similar to the MG 08, but was mounted on a bipod, and though still massive was a good deal lighter. It also had the benefit of a 100 round drum magazine, or '*trommel*' officially known as the *Patronenkasten 16*, which contained the belt, making for more convenient handling and traversing. Though not as stable or accurate as a weapon mounted on a full blown sledge mount or tripod, the new machine gun was sighted to 1900 metres. This was doubtless an exaggeration of its realistic capability, but even so it was practical to several hundred metres. It was also provided with a carrying strap, which, with some difficulty, could be used for 'assault fire' on the move.

The MG 08/15 was regarded as a weapon which could go anywhere the infantry went, and was soon pivotal in small unit tactics, as a contemporary German instructions explained, 'For mobile

The 'new model' 7.6 cm light trench mortar and crew, pictured August 1917. Light mortars formed an integral part of many assault units and could be man hauled on small wheels by means of dragging straps. The normal detachment was a *Trupp* of a couple of NCOs and four or five men. This group includes one NCO distinguished by his collar braid and peaked cap, and a signaller with field telephone. Note how the weapon is fired by means of a pull on the lanyard. *SB*

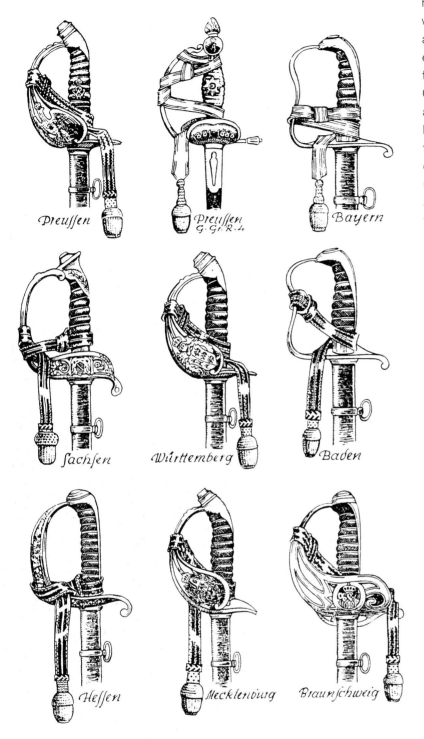

Preußen

Preußen
G. Gr. R. 1.

Bayern

Sachsen

Württemberg

Baden

Hessen

Mecklenburg

Braunschweig

Line drawing of the various sword types carried by officers of the different German states.

defence, the 08/15 is indispensable. It is posted either in the foremost line, or in front of the latter in nests and in shell holes. In the attack, when skilfully handled and judiciously posted, it contributes a valuable increase to the volume of fire. It can advance with the first wave of the assault and engage portions of the enemy's trenches where the attack is held up. This demands initiative. Command, as regards both tactical employment and ammunition resupply, should be exercised by the infantry company commander. Only under these conditions can full use be made of this very excellent weapon.' Production of the new gun was under way in 1916, but it would be 1917 before an appreciable number were in service at the front. Priority of issue was made in the Verdun and other active sectors.

In 1916, British tanks were initially met with panic and consternation, and were only combated by artillery bombardment, or brave individuals prepared to rush them with grenades. Before long, however, a number of weapons had been devised to deal with tanks: these included armour piercing 'K' bullets, and concentrated charges made from several stick grenade heads. Only in 1918 did the infantry begin to receive a weapon with which they could tackle tanks from a range at which they had a realistic chance of survival. This new gun was the Mauser 'T' or *Tank Gewehr*: the first anti-tank rifle. The *T-Gewehr* was a massive single shot bolt action weapon, which one man could just about haul, and it fired a 13 mm round. Its performance was limited, but nevertheless it brought a new tactical dimension to the battlefield.

Flamethrowers could also prove effective both against tanks, and as an assault weapon in their own right. In this technology the Germans were early leaders, having patented a military flamethrower in the first years of the century. A good idea of their description and capabilities was given by one on the receiving end of a flame attack at Ypres in 1917: 'Under cover of the hurly burly of shelling on our plateau and the thick mist, the enemy had concentrated a number of trench mortars against our segment of the line. They pounded it lavishly for ten minutes. Then the defenders suddenly saw advancing towards them a wave of fire. The enemy were attacking under cover of Flammenwerfer, hose pipes leading to petrol tanks carried on the backs of men. When the nozzles were lighted, they threw out a roaring, hissing flame twenty to thirty feet long, swelling at the end to an oily rose, six feet in diameter. Under protection of these hideous weapons the enemy surrounded the pill box, stormed it and killed the garrison.'

The main firearms of the infantry at the end of the Great War. Left, the *Gewehr 98* **demonstrating the five round charger loading system: and centre the MG 08/15 light machine gun, seen here without ammunition.**
P. Hannon

POLITICAL STORMTROOPER

The end of the Great War came suddenly as the Central Powers collapsed like a house of cards, sweeping away with them Imperial houses which had stood the test of centuries. Kaiser Karl of Austria approached President Wilson for peace in mid September: Bulgaria capitulated a few days afterwards. A month later Italian offensives coincided with Czechoslovak and Polish declarations of independence, Army revolts, and the arrival of Spanish influenza in Vienna. The Austrians signed an Armistice on 2 November which came into effect 48 hours later.

In the West, the German Army was still on foreign soil, yet the last hundred days had seen her strength depleting ever faster than it could be replaced. What had been more than five million men had shrunk to four as spring turned to summer; and more German soldiers died in 1918 than any other year of the war. Exactly which straw it was that broke the camel's back has long been debated, yet a combination of factors made the continuation of the war impossible. Long term blockade, first by the Royal Navy, then by the US Navy, led to a long slow strangulation that an indiscriminate U-Boat offensive had in the end only made worse. Supplies of rubber and metals, oils, and foods had dried up one after another until 'Turnip Winters' turned to seasons when little or nothing was available. Many exotic *Ersatz* foodstuffs had appeared, based on things like acorns and nettles, but by late 1918 people were starving in the streets.

The Army may still have been fighting on the battlefield but at best it was a fighting retreat with no prospect of reverse. The British, having inflicted a heavy blow on the so-called 'black day' of 8 August, were now advancing steadily, practising a home grown version of the new infantry tactics. Not to be outdone, US forces, which were now gaining rapidly in strength, were co-operating actively with the French so that there would be no respite in the Meuse and Argonne. Tanks, which were once blithely dismissed as of nuisance and morale value only, were now appearing on the Allied inventory in massive numbers. By the last month, less than 50 German and captured machines were facing about 3000 armoured vehicles.

Ludendorff veered from pessimism to the optimistic belief that the Army could at least defend the boundaries of the Reich. He concurred with Hindenburg that a cessation of hostilities was necessary, and on the home front Prince Max of Baden was appointed the new German Chancellor with a view both to establishing a new elected government and to seeking peace. When Ludendorff attempted to dictate negotiation of the peace to Prince Max, his bluff was finally called. The Kaiser accepted Ludendorff's resignation, and, though Hindenburg was retained, Prince Max promptly fell ill. The final seal on disintegration was set by the Imperial German Navy. For whilst peace overtures had been launched as early as the first week of October, the uneven struggle dragged on. In this atmosphere of pessimism and desperation Admiral Hipper decided to launch a major 'do or die' sortie against the British Grand Fleet. The result was a mutiny on 29 October, which spread ashore to Kiel, and then like wildfire along the North Sea, so that by 6 November the coastal regions were all but paralysed. The *Burgfrieden*, or 'social peace', which had helped unite much of the country behind the war was now breaking down. As a left wing saying of the period put it, an end to the war would only be possible 'when the bullets are aimed in the opposite direction'. Two days later, an Armistice was agreed which would come into effect at 11am on 11 November. Thus was born out of turmoil the *Dolchstosslegende*, the perception of the Army and future Nationalists that the war had been lost through a 'stab in the back'.

Even the preliminary terms of the Armistice effectively emasculated German forces. The Rhineland was to be evacuated, and in addition to the loss of her Navy and Airforce, 5,000 artillery pieces, 25,000 machine guns and 3,000 trench

Helft uns siegen!

zeichnet
Kriegsanleihe

Above, going home, 1918. The demobilisation of a vast army, half starved, discontented by defeat, and facing economic hardship in an unstable new republic, helped lead to the build up of new political pressures.
SB

Right, the post Versailles German nightmare as explained in Zimmermann's *Soldatenfibel*; surrounded by potential enemies, yet limited to an army of 100,000.

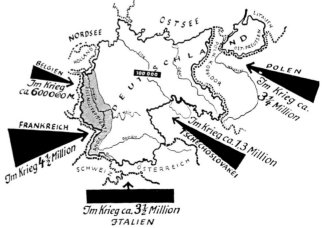

mortars were handed over. The Treaty of Versailles in June the following year would only serve to reinforce this position. The Kaiser, now in exile in Holland, and leading generals and admirals were declared war criminals. The German Army was to be reduced to 100,000 officers and men, and to prevent this from being easy to expand, terms of service were set at minimums of 25 and 12 years respectively for officers and men. At least this tiny rump was able to claim quality, and there was little obsolete equipment, because there was little equipment allowed.

An unfortunate side effect of the restrictions on the Army was that the forces of law and order available to the fledgling democratic government were totally insufficient to deal with anarchy and the varied revolutionary forces which were unleashed in the aftermath of war. The union of states which was Germany itself threatened to break apart. In Berlin, in January 1919, there was an attempted coup, which was only savagely crushed after street fighting and intervention from General von Lüttwitz's *Freikorps*. Disorder continued sporadically for a couple of months. In Munich, a left wing 'Central Council' or Soviet under Ernst Niekisch seized power, and was only defeated by a combination of *Reichswehr* and independent *Freikorps* forces under Ritter von Epp in May 1919. The fact that many of the left wing leadership were Jewish, and modelled their efforts on the Bolsheviks, was doubly disastrous for democracy. One effect was an increase in sympathy for the many right wing parties which now sprang up and another was an increase in anti-Semitism.

In view of the relative impotence of the government, and despite their excesses, the *Freikorps* came to be viewed as protectors against confusion and a patriotic force, in the same way as their nineteenth century namesakes who had fought against Napoleon. In the absence of sufficient legitimate troops they were used to help drive Communists from the Baltic states, and to protect Upper Silesia from the Poles. It was almost as if the war, in a reversal of the Clausewitzian dictum, was now being carried on by political means. Thus it was that bodies like von Epps *Einwohnerwehr*, the officers' league *Eiserne Faust* and the *Deutschvölkische Schutz und Trutzbund* gained a credibility unthinkable in other times. The result has fairly been described as a 'brutalisation of German politics'.

THE SA AND SS

The influence of the Stormtrooper experience, and of the war in general on inter-war politics, is difficult to exaggerate, especially at the extremes of the German political spectrum. As Ernst Jünger put it from a right wing perspective, 'the whole nation was shot through by the single feeling of being one race, one in flesh and blood, one in the consciousness of presenting an undivided front to the outside world'. Former front line soldiers perceived themselves as a 'brotherhood' with 'an inner bond', a *Männerbund*.

At the same time there were some who had had all their education through the war and were essentially good for 'nothing but hurling bombs'. These 'true types of primitive life' were often those who were unemployed or unemployable back in civilian life. It was all too easy, using the right

Next page, the political Stormtrooper as a pillar of the new order: postcards commemorating the SA Reich competitions of 1938, and the Nürnberg (Nuremberg) party day of 1934. *SB*

Above from left to right :
Feldmarschall Mackensen, General Ludendorff, Reichspresident Paul von Hindenburg and General von Seeckt head of the *Reichswehr* at the Tannenberg memorial.
Such public events helped emphasise the continuity between the old army and the new, and the importance of the military as a traditional force for stability in German society.

Reichsparteitag Nürnberg 1934

SA

von Axster-Heudtlaß
SA-Sturmhauptführer

Reichswettkämpfe
Berlin, 15.-17. Juli 1938

rhetoric, to interest such men in newly emergent political movements, especially in the face of an apparent threat from Communism. Very often they did not regard themselves as involved in politics, but as part of a 'militant ideological group' in 'parties above parties', and for them the militaristic aspect of the cult of 'leader' or Führer would have a special appeal especially when delivered by the rising political figure of Adolf Hitler. It was no accident that Hitler's political testament should go under the title of *My Struggle* or *My Battle*.

The muscular brown shirted enforcers of the new National Socialist German Worker's Party; the 'Stormtroopers' of the 'Storm Detachment', or *Sturmabteilung*, were founded in 1921. This body was essentially the work of Ernst Röhm and Hans-Ulrich Klintzsch, and drew heavily on the old *Freikorps*. It would soon outnumber the army of the state, being at the same time an instrument of terror and a bastion against Communism. Its other activities included sports and military style training alongside political indoctrination. Though widely regarded as the lesser of two evils, it was equally worrying to the NSDAP hierarchy, as to the army, that the SA might eventually itself become a 'people's army' supplanting the traditional German armed forces.

An embryonic answer to the overweening SA lay in the leader's personal protectors, the tiny *Stosstrupp Adolf Hitler,* which had marched in the attempted *Putsch* in Munich in 1923. This Praetorian guard within the mass were a restricted bodyguard, enlisted without conditions, who would march even 'against their own brothers'. From 1925 this gradually expanding army within an army would be called the 'Protection Squad' or *Schutzstaffel*, otherwise known as the SS, and after 1934 with the purging of the SA and the assassination of Ernst Röhm, the SS became a significant independent force. The military-political circle would be completed a few months later when the 'Political Readiness Detachments' of the SS were reorganised into 'battalions' for military use. These *Verfügungstruppe*, or special purpose troops, were officially renamed *Waffen SS* in 1940.

Interestingly, though the idea of 'assault detachments' and 'shock troops' remained current in the military, the army proper did not itself keep any permanent formation of soldiers called 'Stormtroopers', preferring instead traditional, and less politically loaded titles such as Rifleman, Pioneer, Fusilier and Grenadier. This was much in keeping with the principle that, prior to 1933, professional soldiers were not allowed to be involved in politics. Nevertheless the important lessons learned in the Great War were far from wasted, and the army would soon be adding more teeth to the 'all arms' approach. The term 'Stormtrooper' would continue to be indiscriminately applied by the Allied press to German assault troops whatever their proper designations.

SA cyclists march past the Führer, Dortmund 1933.

NEW WAYS OF WAR

1918 marked the culmination of a revolution in tactics, and even the advent of a new way of thinking about war. As Ernst Jünger put it, in retrospect, 'A leader of troops today sees very little of his men in the sea of smoke, and cannot compel them to be heroes if they prefer to live for ever... He must be able to rely on them ; and he can only do so if he has trained them to take the initiative rather than to act as puppets... They must certainly be schooled in an iron school if they are to be real men, but they must be taught to face death with a higher sense of their own responsibility than in former days. We have to free ourselves more and more from drill in massed movements; for since the development of mechanical weapons the functions of massed troops devolve more and more upon individuals. The most essential task today is to educate the soldier so that he can stand on his own with machine gun without losing sight of the engagement as a whole. We shall be able to replace platoons by machine guns, companies by tanks, cavalry regiments by air squadrons, and to rely,

indeed, entirely on the machine – but only if we can count upon a high grade of specialist. For as Xenophon said when he encouraged his infantry to withstand cavalry, " all that occurs in battle is done by men".

The ideal was therefore a highly trained army of specialists imbued with the will to win, an intelligent system of combat, an ability to fight as individuals, and a significant offensive power which could call on a variety of modern machines and technologies. Just how to match such aspirations with the reality of an interwar German army smaller than that of Belgium was the problem which fell largely to General Hans von Seeckt; head of the *Truppenamt* of the Ministry of War from 1919 to 1926. In essence, it was accepted that a 100,000 man army was no practical proposition. Instead this minuscule force was regarded merely as a nucleus or a cadre

Experimenting with towed anti-tank guns and lorry borne troops during the manoeuvres of 1932. Tanks would only be fully effective when closely supported by mobile infantry, artillery, and engineers.
IWM Q71395

Next page, a comparative study in camouflage during the great autumn exercise of 1936. The addition of only a few leaves to the steel helmet renders the men furthest from the camera practically invisible amongst the vegetable crop. Note the MG 08/15 machine gun and the helmet bands.
IWM HU 54959

Realistic assault troop training; the helmets and rifles
are of obsolete types.
IWMMH 1924

onto which would be grafted a mass of newly raised men in the event of emergency. Thus was born the idea of a *Führerarmee*, literally an army of leaders. Private soldiers would receive training making them capable of acting as NCOs; in turn the NCOs were treated as officers in the making; whilst junior officers were expected to be able to assume the responsibilities of higher command. In the event of war, the peacetime army could be expected to do no more than act as a temporary shield, allowing mobilisation to take place before it was too late. Smallness could even be turned to advantage in some instances, because a few men were easier to re-equip or retrain than a mass. Political resistance to change and innovation was also easier to overcome when politicians were aware that the army was numerically inferior to the task.

Whilst the French drew from the Great War an appreciation of the power of static defences, concrete, and tanks in close and localised support, German tacticians learnt very different lessons. What really impressed them was being on the receiving end of armour; the frustration of drawn out campaigns and supplies which failed; and offensives which were tied to rail links and the speed of plodding horses. The answer appeared to lie with tanks with greater range, and battle groups which attempted to combine the advantages of tanks, infantry and artillery supported by air power. As early as 1921, there were experiments in the Harz mountains in which infantry travelled in requisitioned civilian lorries. These humble beginnings would be the precursors of the motorised infantry battalions which would accompany the Panzers.

The Germans studied the methods of other powers, and a particular object of research were those British officers who believed that armour could be better applied than in the First World War, most notably Major, later General, J.F.C. Fuller. As early as 1922, agreement was reached by which German experts would help to set up munitions factories in the Soviet Union, and in return they would be able to operate training grounds at Lipetsk, a gas school at Samara, and later a tank training centre at Kazan. Within five years a new prototype tank was under development, concealed under the cover story of a piece of agricultural machinery. The withdrawal of the Allied Control Commission in 1928 allowed more activity to take place in relative security on German soil.

A prime mover in the evolution of the new offensive methods was Captain Heinz Guderian, an officer in the Transport Troops Inspectorate. Importantly, though a tank enthusiast, Guderian realised that it was only the synthesis of the power of armour with the more traditional virtues of all the other arms which would produce a winning formula. By the end of the 1920s, he had concluded by means of the study of history, British methods, and German exercises with mock-ups of armoured vehicles that, 'tanks would never be able to produce their full effect until the other weapons on whose support they must inevitably rely were brought up to

A photograph from the collection of Generaloberst Ritter von Lieb, showing 15th Division negotiating a pontoon bridge over the Werra during the exercises of 1937. Note that the men in the foreground have light assault equipment consisting of a blanket or tent section wrapped around a mess tin. The double sided red and yellow reversible helmet band, or *Helmband 32*, enabled umpires to identify forces. One man, centre, carries the MG 08/15 light machine gun.
IWM HU 54967

their standard of speed and cross country performance. In such a formation of all arms, the tanks must play the primary role, the other arms being subordinated to the requirements of the armour. It would be wrong to include tanks in infantry divisions: what was needed were armoured divisions which would include all the supporting arms needed to allow tanks to fight to full effect'. Manoeuvres using an imaginary division of Panzers took place in 1929. In 1931, Guderian was appointed to command 3rd (Prussian) Motorised Battalion, a mixed formation comprising a reconnaissance company of armoured cars, a company of dummy tanks, an anti-tank company and a motor cycle company, though at this time the *Reichswehr* had only about ten genuine tanks.

Guderian was highly fortunate in that his ideas would coincide very closely with the opinions of the new Führer. Hitler's own view was that armies were assembled for war, not for peace; and that they should be capable of projecting national aspiration. Wars would only be started by the new National Socialist regime when it was clear that an already demoralised enemy would succumb quickly to ' a single gigantic stroke'. More specifically Hitler

fervently believed that the 'next war will be quite different to the last... Infantry attacks and mass formations are obsolete. Interlocked frontal struggles lasting for years on petrified fronts will not return'. Properly handled open warfare was not only an objective, but a guarantee of offensive superiority.

By 1934, Hitler had effectively cast aside the provisions of Versailles intending both to expand the army to over 20 divisions and to cut the period of conscription so as to train a wider segment of the population. That same year the first real tank battalion was completed, under the cover designation 'Motor Transport Training Unit'. Even the critics of the expensive tank forces allowed that tanks had a role to play along with Storm troops, and this combined arms approach was a significant facet of General Beck's 1933 pamphlet *Die Truppenführung*.

In 1935, Beck was created Chief of the General Staff, a fact which perhaps balanced the over optimistic views of the tank enthusiasts, and made sure that there would be plenty of assault trained infantry to exploit the dramatic advances of the Panzers. Similarly influential was the publication of Erwin Rommel's 1937 *Infanterie Greift An* which stressed both the roles of assault infantry, and mountain troops through the study of Great War experiences. It also proved a considerable fillip to Rommel's career, helping to propel him from infantry tactics instructor at Dresden Military Academy to Potsdam and thence to commander of the *Führerhauptquartier*, or headquarters, in the event of war.

So it was that the training of the foot soldiers, though never as glamorous as their mounted or armoured colleagues, was not neglected in the interwar period. A number of new manuals, amongst them Bodo Zimmerman's *Die Soldatenfibel*, helped to show the current state of knowledge and training. The infantry section of 13, including a leader, was now firmly regarded as a significant minor tactical

Men of the 'Band of the Red Banner', Hamburg 9 November 1918. The stirrings of revolution in northern Germany were the last straw for the Second Empire. On this very day the Generals informed Kaiser Wilhelm that the army would no longer fight for him. The group of revolutionaries seen here includes both a seaman and soldiers who have removed the cockades from their caps. *SB*

significant minor tactical unit. It was divided into two sub sections: one a light machine gun *Trupp* of four men with either the MG 08/15 or MG 13 type weapon; the other sub section a *Schützentrupp*, of eight riflemen inclusive of their own junior NCO. Nine such sections made up a 'rifle' company, whilst three rifle companies plus a machine gun company of 12 heavy machine guns made up the battalion. In offensive action, the sections had two basic common deployments: a scattered firing line; and a formation in which the machine gun *Trupp* positioned itself so as to assist the advance of the rifles, in loose single file or scattered, by fire and movement.

Officer training stressed tactics and the leading of infantry battalions in combat; a subject which was even taught to officers of other branches of the service. Siegfried Knappe attended officer training at the *Kriegsschule* in Potsdam, where; 'Our training began immediately and continued without letup until Christmas. We studied only military subjects, because we were all gymnasium [senior, or grammar school] graduates who had just completed thirteen years of academic studies. Our major subject was tactics, and we spent most of our time on it. Other subjects included topography and reading maps, engineering (mostly building and blowing up bridges), basic artillery, horseback riding, drilling on the parade ground with rifles, cooperation with the Luftwaffe, and physical education. we spent six hours in the classroom and three hours in the field. We learned everything an infantry battalion commander had to know in any kind of precombat or combat situation.'

By 1936, there were three Panzer divisions, and each comprised three medium and one light tank battalion, but these were put together with two motorised infantry battalions, two light howitzer battalions, and a battalion each of motor cycle, anti-tank, and reconnaissance troops to create a balanced force. There were also experiments with divisions made up purely of motorised troops, and with tank brigades earmarked for infantry support, though Guderian regarded these as a dissipation of the available strength. Beck also insisted that manoeuvres accommodated the mass of the infantry who were set to lengthy marches on foot.

From 1936 to 1938, the Spanish Civil War formed a practical testing ground for theory, with Colonel von Thoma's small force committed to the Nationalist side. Eventually four tank battalions would serve in Spain, yet there seemed to be worrying indicators that tank defence could be made more effective than tank attack. When German troops moved into Austria as a result of the *Anschluss* of 1937, no less than 30 % of the armoured vehicles suffered mechanical failures despite a total lack of armed opposition. A graphic indicator that tanks alone were not a wonder weapon. Interestingly, German theorists also began to consider the role of tanks and aircraft in mobile defence, and von Leeb amongst others came to the conclusion that motorised forces would be valuable in preventing the defensive war breaking down into the sort of stalemate which had occurred in the Great War. It was not without doubts that the Generals faced the prospect of war: doubts about preparedness, and doubts about the cult of the tank.

Above, happy times circa 1939. This amorous soldier of infantry regiment Nr 9 wears the enlisted ranks dress tunic or *Waffenrock*, complete with marksman's lanyard. Such ceremonial frippery would seldom be seen after the outbreak of war. *SB*

Next page, Freikorps personnel with Erhardt armoured car and flamethrower, on the streets of Berlin during the 1919 rising. Some of the men wear the peakless steel helmet which had been destined for export to the Turks prior to the end of the Great War. *TRH Pictures*

BLITZKRIEG STORMTROOPER

Despite advances in armoured warfare at the start of World War Two, the role of infantry remained critical. As the handbook *Dienst Unterricht in Unser Heer* put it: 'In collaboration with other arms the infantry gains the decision in battle, captures enemy positions and holds them. It conducts close combat actions so as to destroy the enemy.'

The infantry regiment of 1940 consisted of three battalions, plus regimental headquarters; regimental headquarters company; a howitzer company or *Infanterie-Geschütz Kompanie*; and an anti-tank company or *Panzer-Jäger Kompanie*. Though German planning aimed at rapid success the vast majority of the regimental transport was horse drawn, as each regiment had just 73 motor vehicles and 47 motor cycles, but 210 vehicles, carts, wagons, and field kitchens drawn by 683 horses. Despite suggestions by senior generals such as Fromm and Guderian that all, or part, of the ordinary infantry division should be motorised, many units would remain reliant on horses until the end of the war. When railways ran out, the ordinary *Landser* was indeed expected to expend sweat and boot leather.

The main fighting unit was the infantry battalion consisting of three 'rifle' companies and a 'machine gun' company. Each infantry company was itself composed of three 'platoons', plus a company headquarters and an anti-tank rifle section. Originally each platoon was broken down into three sections known as Gruppe, but after the Polish campaign, platoons were reorganised so that there were four sections, each having a section commander, plus nine men and a light machine gun. The platoon also had its own 50mm light mortar and two man crew. In the machine gun, or support company, there were not only three 'heavy' machine gun platoons, each of four machine guns, in two sections of two, but a mortar platoon with two 81mm mortars. The 'heavy' machine guns were often MG 34 weapons set up on sustained fire tripods, but in second line units they could also be the old MG 08, or captured types.

Though shortages, and the understandable desire to bring to bear as much hardware as possible could upset the standard system, each section was supposed to comprise a commander armed with a machine pistol (usually the MP 38 or MP 40); a three man light machine gun party whose main armament was the MG 34; and five riflemen armed with the Mauser Kar 98k. As well as leading the section in combat and directing the fire of his men, the section commander or squad leader was responsible for the unit's weapon serviceability, and the immediate supply of weapons and stores. The combat manual left the reader in no doubt of the importance, and the responsibilities, of the squad leader : 'The *Gruppenführer* must be an example – and a combat example – for his men. The most effective means for gaining the confidence and respect of subordinates and for getting most out of them is to set an example. But in order to set an example, the *Gruppenführer* must have a stronger will than his men, must do more than they do and must himself always discharge his duties and obey orders cheerfully... In order to be a leader in the field, a superior must display an exemplary bearing before his men in the moment of danger, and be willing, if necessary, to die for them.' Yet *in extremis* any soldier was expected to be able to lead. As one war time divisional commander put it: 'He whose heart is in the right place, can and should lead even without shoulder straps and stripes'.

The three men of the light machine gun team had specific tasks and burdens. The 'Nr 1' fired the machine gun and took care of its maintenance. He carried not only the weapon but a small tool bag, an entrenching tool and pistol. Like the section commander, he was also supposed to take with him into action sun glasses, torch, gas mask, and emergency rations. When the MG 34 was used from its 'light' bipod mount the gunners were taught to fire in short bursts, or *Feuerstösse*, thus avoiding

overheating and running short of ammunition too quickly in the fire fight.

The second man of the machine gun team directly assisted the gunner, looking after the next four magazines or belts to be fired, helping to adjust the bipod, clear stoppages or change barrels. Much of his personal kit was intended to be identical with that of the gunner with the exception that he carried an ammunition box and a spare gun barrel. The third man in the team was designated ammunition carrier, bringing with him two ammunition boxes in addition to his rifle, entrenching tool, gas mask and iron ration. In action it was his duty to lie under cover to the rear of the gunner with ammunition and magazines ready for the assistant to pick up.

The remaining five riflemen of the *Gruppe* were all intended to carry their entrenching tools, gas masks and rations in action, but could also be detailed to carry greater or lesser numbers of hand and smoke grenades, explosive charges, ammunition, and even the machine gun sustained fire tripod. The most senior of the riflemen was designated as deputy section commander, or *Stellvertretender Gruppenführer*, and to him fell the duty of assisting, or if necessary replacing, the section commander. The deputy was also responsible for keeping in touch with neighbouring sections and the platoon commander. On the march the sections made use of the 'platoon cart' on which were carried the machine guns, 50mm mortar, ammunition, grenades, camouflage stores and other heavy baggage.

BATTALION DEPLOYMENT

At the start of any contact it was usual for the battalion commander to come up to the front line, and, after a brief reconnaissance, establish his 'battle' headquarters in a position where good observation could be had of the likely epicentre of any action. The ideal place was concealed, yet had good communications, and covered approaches whereby runners could reach the headquarters without either becoming casualties or giving away the location of the post. It was useful to have artillery and other observation posts nearby, but none so close as to make a dangerous bunch of potential targets. Likewise it was thought convenient to have the battalion 'signal office' and the remainder of the headquarters in the vicinity, but at least fifty metres from the place where the commanding officer and his adjutant were working. Further to the rear, well beyond the signal office, an aid post would be established by the medical officer. Frontages had to be adjusted according to terrain and necessity, but ideally a battalion would be deployed across 400 to 800 metres; a company on a 200 to 250 metre sector; and a platoon on a distance of 100 to 250 metres.

From his forward position, the battalion commander would attempt to run the local battle: written orders were extremely rare, but when they were required they were prepared by the adjutant, who also made any sketches, gathered any information needed for the war diary, and transmitted instructions down the chain of command. Battle instructions were passed first to the company headquarters: they would be acted on

Left, an assault engineer section ready for action against a fortified position, near Saar, August 1940. The two men in the foreground carry smoke canisters, and have wire cutters, pistols, grenades and *Sprengpatronen* demolition charges at their belts. Further down the line are men equipped with *Sprengkorper 28* charges, pole charges, and concentrated charges, a couple carry rifles to cover the wire cutting, smoke, and demolition teams.

Above, crossing the Meuse in a small assault boat or *Kleine Flossack*, 1940. Boats were usually operated by the *Pionere*, or assault engineers, and where possible smaller pneumatic boats would be towed across water by larger 'storm boats'. The first teams across would usually set up ropes so that more men could be pulled across; later, pontoon bridges would be established.

1936 Spanien 1939

Großdeutschland

Führerhauptquartier

Brandenburg

by the company commander, whilst the senior NCO there would attempt to maintain visual communication back and forward, to battalion and platoon level respectively. Also at each company headquarters were three orderlies, a couple of cyclists for company communications, and a bugler who would carry the company commander's machine pistol whilst he was otherwise engaged. The anti-tank rifle section was often employed in the vicinity of the company headquarters, each gunner present being accompanied by an ammunition holder. Company transport was normally grouped together and hidden away under cover looked after by an NCO. At local level the platoon commander was usually assisted by a platoon sergeant who carried a signal pistol for firing coloured flares. Certain members of the company or platoon headquarters might also be detailed as observers, orderlies, or 'air sentries' whose duty was to scan the sky for aircraft.

Whenever the opportunity arose there would be the closest possible liaison with tanks, aircraft, and nearby battalions. As the 'German Army Yearbook' of 1937 had put it, 'in each combat only the closest cooperation of all services can achieve success'. Commanders would be aided not only by conventional radio and field telephones, but by the provision of recognition flags, light signals and

ground strips. These ground strips, placed so as to be visible to friendly aircraft, were white on one side but had a red backing to be shown in snowy conditions.

The formations adopted by small units depended on situation, and were intended to have flexibility, yet the section was almost always operated as a group, and only split up under exceptional circumstances. In the advance, two deployments were usual: single file or *Reihe*, and extended or open order line, a 'chain' formation, referred to as the *Kette*. When approaching the enemy in a loose single file it was usual for the section commander to take the 'point', followed at a short interval by the machine gun team. The remainder of the squad strung out behind, with the senior rifleman bringing up the rear. Extended line made the section more obvious to the enemy but had the advantage in that all the weapons of the group could be brought to bear. In this formation the machine gun team formed up to the centre or flank, and the rifles formed a ragged, staggered line with the men five or so paces apart, taking whatever advantage of the ground was available. The senior rifleman took position to one flank, but the section commander was again expected to lead from the front. When a whole platoon operated together it usually adopted an 'arrowhead' formation with a couple of sections

Opposite, Unteroffizier Russia 1941. The central figure shows an infantry *Unteroffizier* squad leader, during Operation Barbarossa, Russia, 1941. The uniform is the 1935 type *Feldbluse* with dark green collar and shoulder straps and four pleated patch pockets. The belt equipment features magazine pouches for the MP 38 and pistol holster. Other items carried include two stick grenades, binoculars, and a machine gun ammunition belt. An Iron Cross First Class and wound badge are worn on the left breast. Jack boots or *Marschsteifel*, and the M35 steel helmet complete the ensemble. The neck cloth is a typical private purchase embellishment.

The breast eagle, centre top, is of the type worn on the right breast by the army in the early part of World War Two. It is shown over the Waffen SS eagle which was displayed on the left upper arm. To the left the three insignia are the *Edelweiss* arm badge of the mountain troops; regimental standard bearer's arm shield (*Jäger*

regiment); and the infantry assault badge. The infantry assault badge, which shows a rifle with fixed bayonet, was instituted in December 1939: in silver it denotes participation in three or more infantry assaults, counter attacks, or armed reconnaissances. The four circular trade and proficiency badges, shown centre left, are the monogram of the *Gasschützunteroffizier* or 'gas defence NCO'; the snake and staff of medical personnel; the technician's cog wheel; and the crossed rifles of the ordnance NCO. All of these were worn on the lower right sleeve; artillery and *Nebelwerfer* badges were worn on the left.

The set of equipment, seen top right, is the *Pioniersturmgepäck*, which was carried by a proportion of assault engineers from 1941 onward. It was designed to accomodate explosive charges, fuses, grenades, and small arms ammunition. There was a space at the top for a mess tin, and at the front on the wearer's right side, a gas mask.

The bayonet and water bottle are seen carried on the belt.

The rifle, left, is the Kar 98k, 7.92 mm rifle, fitted with a small *Zielfernrohr* telescopic sniper sight. At the top is seen the single shot *Panzerbüchse 38* anti-tank rifle which was capable of penetrating about 30 mm of armour at 100 metres: this saw service in Poland but was rapidly supplanted by the *Panzerbüchse 39*. Centre right is the Italian 9mm Beretta 1938A sub-machine gun, which also saw service with German forces as the *Maschinenpistole* (Beretta) 38 (i). Next to the Beretta is seen the 3kg *Heft Hohladung* anti-tank magnetic mine (c 1942); this was dangerous to use but could deal with most AFVs if well placed. The light mortar, bottom left, is the 5 cm *Granatwerfer 36*. Usually crewed by two men it provided valuable platoon support with rapid fire to 500 metres.

Four uniform cuff titles are seen lower left. That at the top was instituted on

21 June 1939, and was worn on the right forearm to commemorate service with the Condor Legion during the Spanish Civil War. Red and gold were the colours of Nationalist Spain. The *Spanien* cuff insignia was the first of several campaign titles, which also included AFRIKA in silver grey on khaki for North African service, and KRETA in yellow on white for the invasion of Crete. The *Großdeutschland* title in green was granted to members of the elite infantry regiment in 1939; a version with a black backing was later used for the Panzer division of the same name. The *Führerhauptquatier* cuff title seen here was in use from c. 1939 by all ranks responsible for the personal safety of the Führer and his headquarters. The *Brandenburg* cuff title was introduced in 1936 for the second SS *Totenkopf-Standarte*. It was one of many worn by the Waffen SS yet the Brandenburg name had a distinguished history, having previously been used by various regiments of the Prussian army.

The small tank badge worn on the right upper arm was instituted in March 1942 and signified single handed destruction of a fighting vehicle. A gold class of this badge for five such kills was introduced in 1943.

The four shoulder straps shown bottom right are as follows: soldier of *Infanterie Regiment 109* old style with pointed end, manufactured between 1934 and 1938 and still in use at the outbreak of war; *Unteroffizier* of local defence battalion 606, manufactured post 1940; *Oberfeldwebel* of infantry *Grenadier Regiment 107*, note the two red *Balken* denoting second battalion a system unique to *34 Infanterie Division*: and the officer's strap is of a *Leutnant* of *Skijäger Regiment Nr 1*. Painting by Richard Hook

perhaps fifty yards or more out to either flank of the direction of movement, and the remainder of the sections strung out one behind another in the centre. In the advance it was instructed that a loose but narrow formation be maintained as long as possible so that supporting machine guns assisting from the rear could keep up their fire unobstructed.

ATTACK

Offensive action was assumed to be the most productive and in stressing its significance, the combat manual made a direct link between the Stormtrooper of the Great War and the contemporary assault infantryman: 'The offensive implies a feeling of superiority. The attacker has the initiative; he determines where and when the battle will be fought. Superiority in numbers is not always the decisive factor. Superiority in leadership, in the capacity of the troops... in surprise effect and in quick, active seizure and exploitation of favourable opportunities may lead to complete success against a numerically superior enemy. The World War presented many examples of this.'

It was expected that the company and platoon commanders should fight at the sharp end, exercising close control and keeping the action in view, where necessary entering the battle at the decisive place 'regardless' of their own person.

Company commanders were expected to direct whatever support weapons they had been allotted, whilst platoon commanders were to detail localised reserves. The key to a successful attacking battle was often the *Feuerkampf*, or fire fight, in which fire superiority was progressively gained on a defined sector; frequently in three distinct phases. These were the *Niederhalten* or pinning down of the opposition with mortars and machine guns : followed by *blinden*, – blinding the defence; and the *Niederkampfen* or concentrated fire from all available support weapons under which the attacking troops would fight their way into the enemy position.

The advance to contact was carried out in bounds by the designated attacking units, from one visible objective to another, with the next objective specified as soon as the lead troops had reached the preceding one. Where serious resistance was encountered these bounds would become fully fledged fire and movement, but section commanders were cautioned not to open fire with the machine guns until forced to by the ground and enemy fire. Once a fire fight began to develop in the front line, it was likely to become obvious where the opposition's weak points lay, and here the attack was to be pressed home deep into the enemy position. The platoon commander was supposed to

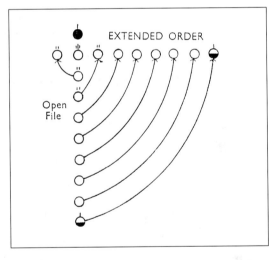

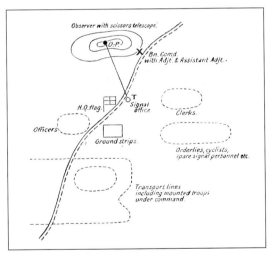

Above left, the single file *Reihe*, and the *Kette* or chain formation commonly adopted by the infantry section, as depicted in *'The German Army of Today'*, 1943.

Above right, layout of a German infantry battalion HQ. *From 'German Infantry in Action'*, 1941.

Opposite, men of SS Motorised Regiment *Germania*, Netherlands 1940. Though trained in similar assault tactics, Waffen-SS troops were distinguished by myriad details of uniform and equipment. Amongst those visible here are the 1937 type *Feldbluse* with eagle on the left arm and *Germania* cuff title,

and the 1935 type steel helmet with double *Siegrunen* insignia on the right side. This device was first drawn by *Sturmhauptführer* Walter Heck, a graphic designer employed by the Hoffstätter company of Bonn, who was paid 2.50 Reichsmarks for the design ! *IWM MH255*

lead by example, maintaining the momentum of the attack. There was to be no attempt to move around the flanks of the enemy until a penetration had been achieved. Such a battalion attack, from first contact to successful outcome, was intended to take less than three quarters of an hour. No time was to be wasted on over elaborate fire plans or lengthy consultations, and no efforts were to be wasted on attempting strictly linear advances: aggressive small group initiatives and infiltrations were to be encouraged.

The final rush to contact was to be made by whole sections, led by the squad leaders. As they dashed forward they were instructed to cheer, and fire all weapons on the move, including the section light machine gun. Such machine gun fire on the move was less than accurate, but it did happen, and was doubtless aided by the fact that the MG 34 would accept drums as well as belts. *Unterscharführer* Hahn described an incident during an assault in which he unleashed four belts, 'mostly from the hip' before a well camouflaged Russian soldier popped up at a range of barely ten metres and shot him twice. The blows from the enemy rounds feeling as though they had 'ripped my legs off'.

Once amongst the opposition the aim was to immediately 'break the enemy's resistance', using not only their rifles and bayonets but pistols and entrenching tools. According to the manual the last word was the, '… vigorous shock power of the rifleman with bayonet which overcomes the enemy. Fine leadership on the part of the squad leader consists in bringing his riflemen into contact with the enemy in as strong a condition as possible. The faster the leader brings his squad forward… without exposing it to unnecessary losses, the greater will be his success. The outcome of the attack will depend on the will of each individual soldier to attack and particularly the will of the leader'. A successful attack was followed by a swift regrouping on the objective, with the machine gun set up in a central position with the riflemen in twos and threes round about, within voice control of the section commander.

If an attack was to be made against a known strong point, it was recommended that a detailed reconnaissance be carried out beforehand, and that the battalion form special assault, or 'storm' detachments. The organisation of an assault detachment was to be flexible depending on the task in hand, but would often consist of a mix and match approach, putting together a number of smaller parties to suit the nature of the objective. A wire cutting party was likely to include three or four personnel for each gap to be cut, and each

of the team would be equipped with either a pistol or rifle in addition to wire cutters, grenades, one hatchet between two, sand bags and explosive charges.

For destroying embrasures, a three man group was recommended, two of them with pistols covered by a rifleman. Their ancillary equipment was to consist of grenades, sand bags, a 3 kg explosive charge, two petrol cans, and a signal pistol. This group could choose to grenade an aperture; blow their own hole in the fortification; or use petrol and set it alight with a round from the flare gun. Flamethrowers might be available if assault engineers were deployed, and could likewise be used on bunkers and embrasures. Smoke parties were ideal to shroud the rest of the assault team, or provide diversions. These groups would consist of two or three men each and would usually be supplied with wire cutters, entrenching tools, and rifles or pistols, as well as smoke grenades or candles. Close support for the wire cutters and embrasure parties would be given by two or three man groups deploying light machine guns, rifles and machine pistols, and provided with communications equipment and grenades as necessary. Section commanders tasked with leading a close assault were expected to carry machine pistols, wire cutters, signal pistol, field glasses, grenades, compass and whistle.

In Russia, Helmut Pabst would describe a real close assault, in this instance by a combat patrol, on a feature known as 'the Dugout Garden': 'They load the machine pistols, buckle on their equipment, grab the bags of grenades, and build up steps in the trench with empty ammunition boxes… Three sergeants and sixteen men press themselves against the parapet ready to jump… The hands of the synchronised watches move towards zero… The fire comes down close to the trench, the black smoke shoots up like a wall, and the infantry jump into the last bursts from their own guns. It's a sudden, wild, movement, a cat-like jumping through treacherous snow, a second of deadly, breathless tension, in which all eyes follow the thin line of men racing through no man's land in great leaps. With the last shell they are in the enemy's trench.

'Like a thunderstorm the patrol is upon them, dividing up and running down both sides of the trench. The first dug outs blow up, machine gun posts erupt, ugly black mushrooms spring up, and the grenades continue the clearing up, small flat explosions spreading ahead. Through splashing dirt and over collapsing brown figures the patrol fight their way. One charge flies into a dug out without exploding. The enemy stream out and fall over one another into the fire of the machine pistol. A

Low technology signalling. An *Unteroffizier* attaches carrier pigeons in panniers onto a messenger dog. The model 1935 field grey *Feldbluse* worn here has dark green collar and shoulder straps edged with rank *Tresse*, and a proficiency badge on the right sleeve. A qualified *Brieftaubenmeister*, or pigeon postmaster, was distinguished by a capital gothic 'B'. The helmet is of the 1918 type with army eagle insignia.
IWM STT 39

grenade does the rest. The men are black in the face. Some are scratched... The enemy assemble for counter attacks. Three are repelled then the patrol disengages itself... With whistling lungs the men fall back into their own trench. The last is Sergeant Major Jakobs. They're all black. Blackened, dirt encrusted, exhausted. A trail of red goes to the aid post. But over on the enemy's side, on a front of two hundred and twenty yards, ten dug outs and twenty machine gun posts have been blown up, eleven heavy machine guns and a 45 mm anti-tank gun destroyed. Seventy to ninety dead are lying in the trench.'

If an assault on a major prepared position proceeded strictly according to text book plan, the artillery and infantry guns would open a swift barrage whilst support machine guns, anti-aircraft guns, tanks, and anti-tank guns directly engaged enemy fortified positions. The guns would then shift to more distant targets allowing machine guns to play on pill boxes and positions as the assault engineers came forward. Smoke and flamethrowers would then envelop the position as demolition teams went to work on obstacles and concrete structures. Next the wire cutters moved forward under smoke and covering fire. As soon as their task was complete, the embrasure attacking parties stormed through the gaps, again covered by

fire and smoke, and went to ground close to the targets. Next the support groups moved up engaging the enemy strong points, and the embrasure attacking groups moved in. Finally the remainder of the battalion would come up, with infantry guns and headquarters relocated to new positions.

Just how close supporting guns could be in such attacks was reported by Leutnant Siegfied Knappe, an artillery officer during the campaign on the Oise in June 1940: 'I was up front with the infantry, and when they asked for help I called for a 105 mm gun from first battery to come up. The infantry commander showed me a house across the canal... from which the French machine guns were firing... We had to have the gun ready to fire, push it around the bend (behind which we were protected by a building), aim, and fire at the machine guns about twenty five metres away before they could get us with their fire. It was not my job to do this, but I wanted to do it to make sure it was effective. Seven of us manned the gun... The crew loaded the gun..."At my command, we will push the gun around the corner, and I will aim the gun and give the order to fire. Everyone understand ?" I looked around and six men nodded...We pushed the gun around the corner of the building at the bend. Pinpoints of light flashed from the machine guns in the basement

Next page, attacking a blockhouse using a 1935 model light flamethrower. Assault order equipment is worn with the mess tin positioned high on the back: the man nearest the camera is holding a flare pistol, which squad leaders were instructed to carry for signalling. *IWM MH 199*

Below, Fox hole defence, France 1940. Note the NCO with distinctive braid around the collar, sacking helmet cover, binoculars, and five round short Kar 98 k carbine. The other weapon visible is the K98b Mauser, a conversion of the old G98 long rifle, quantities of which still remained in service during World War Two.

across the canal as we aimed the gun and jerked the cord. The French had got their rounds off first, and by the time we fired, all seven of us were sprawled on the ground. I knew I had been hit in the left wrist, but I peered across the canal to see if we had knocked out the enemy machine guns. Only smoke now came from the basement where the machine guns had been located, and our infantry were already dashing across the bridge.' Knappe's rewards for his part in the action were an Iron Cross Second Class and a wound badge. The Iron Cross First Class, another wound badge, and an assault badge would follow for similar close support actions in Russia.

The one place close artillery support could not be used was in airborne attacks, but even here many of the other assault techniques would remain the same. The activity of these aerial 'Storm detachments' during the attack in the West, was described by soldier turned *Fallshirmjäger, Oberleutnant* Rudolf Witzig: 'After the fullest use had been made of the training facilities in Hildesheim, the detachment practised attacking strongly defended fortifications in the Sudentenland, and also carried out trial demolitions at Polish installations near Gleiwitz. Lectures at the sapper school at Karlshorst introduced us to the principles of fortress construction. Finally deserters from the Belgian fortifications were interrogated, and we were able to check what we had been learning against the information they supplied... X-Day was several times postponed, but our time was fully occupied in practising new techniques – such as pin point landing with explosives on the airstrip and in the open country, or rapid disembarkation when fully armed. In addition to flamethrowers and collapsible assault ladders which we had built ourselves, the special equipment for the operation consisted chiefly of 2.5 tons of explosives, predominantly cavity charges, which were used for the first time at Eben-Emael for cracking the armoured domes.... The rest of the storm detachment carried the usual arms; six light machine guns, sub machine guns, hand grenades, pistols, smoke bombs, entrenching tools and a radio. A final stroke of ingenuity... was the plan to drop by parachute several groups of uniformed dummies...'

INFANTRY IN DEFENCE

The infantry was the prime means by which ground was held, but it was not intended that positions be defended in a linear manner. German theory of 1940 called for the use of 'defended localities', which were to be 'disposed irregularly and in depth', so as to be mutually supporting. These areas were often laid out for all round defence, and made it possible to continue resistance even when the position had been penetrated, these nests would become known as 'hedgehogs'. Whilst there might be no physical 'line' on the ground it was desirable that the zones of fire interlock, and that within each position there be alternative posts so that troops and weapons could be redeployed locally to meet threats from different directions.

Once the battalion commander had declared his 'main line of resistance', it was the job of the company commanders to organise individual

Above, the lighter side of life: junior NCOs and men carousing at Christmas. Christmas Eve and New Year's Eve figure large in the German festive calendar. Despite National Socialist efforts to replace the word 'Christmas' with 'Yuletide' and stop school carols and nativity plays, the Third Reich did little to blunt popular enthusiasm for a tradition which was made all the more poignant by wartime separations. *SB*

Opposite, infantry pause on the road near Amiens, France 1940. Ordinary German infantry divisions of the period had little motor transport, leaving the foot sloggers to toil under considerable loads in full marching order. Note the piled Kar 98 k carbines in the foreground. *IWM MH 9403*

sectors; showing platoon commanders where their troops were to be deployed; coordinating local fire zones with those of support weapons; and making sure that a reserve was kept. The platoon commanders would then receive their instructions, and would themselves initiate the digging of trenches and weapons pits, including dummy positions if these had been ordered. Frequently defended localities would include outposts beyond the main zone in which would be placed sentries and machine gun teams whose main duties would be to provide early warning of the enemy approach and give surprise bursts of fire which would break up, or slow, an attack before it reached the main position. Attackers would often be forced to deploy prematurely. British observers noted that outposts might be located anything up to 5,000 yards in front of the main positions, and that these were sometimes reinforced with anti-tank guns.

Certainly by 1941, Rommel's *Afrika Korps*, fighting in the open spaces of North Africa, was thinking in terms of the *Pakfront*, defensive positions which mixed anti-tank guns, artillery and infantry in mutual support capable of dealing with enemy armour. As Rommel put it: 'Every defended point must be a complete defensive system in itself. Every weapon must be sited so that it is able to fire in every direction. I visualise the ideal arrangement of such defensive points on these lines: one 88 mm flak gun should be sunk into the ground as deeply as the field of fire permits. From here trenches should radiate in three directions to three points – one a machine gun position, the second a heavy mortar position, and the third a light... anti-aircraft or anti-tank gun... Sufficient water, ammunition and supplies for three weeks must always be available. And every man is to sleep prepared for action... In case of enemy attack, the fire of our arms must completely cover the gap between the defended points. Should the enemy succeed in breaking through the gaps, owing to say bad visibility, every weapon must be in a position to engage towards the rear. Let it be clear there is no such thing as a "Direction, Front", but only a "Direction, Enemy"'.

Mines, where available, could form a valuable adjunct to the defence. These were initially of two major types: the plate shaped Teller or 'T' mine, and the *Schützen* or 'S' mine. The former was aimed against vehicles; the latter, which shot a metre out of the ground before exploding in a cloud of shrapnel balls, was primarily anti-personnel. Wooden *Schü* mines, and *Glass* mines were in use from the middle of the war, and owing to their composition were especially difficult to detect. 'T' mines were often laid in regular belts, but odd mines might be laid outside the normal area to slow

traffic across the front or around the sides of mine fields, and regularity was not to be relied on. Equally clumps of 'S' mines could be laid around the edges of an anti-tank field to discourage infantry. Various other tricks made mine fields all the more deadly: booby traps; laying 'T' mines upside down or on top of one another; dummy fields; and wiring 'S' mines to attractive booty or supplies. Sometimes mines were laid so close that there were sympathetic detonations, with several mines going off at a time. Often the front edges of mine fields were left unmarked, with notices at the rear only. In all instances it was intended that one or more conventional weapons sweep the mined areas making the mines difficult to lift or plot under fire.

When a heavy attack materialised on a defended locality, it was planned that the machine gun outposts would open fire first, often at quite long range on pre-prepared target areas. If the enemy persisted in their advance, it was then the job of the riflemen in the forward positions to defend the flanks of the machine gunners. Eventually it might become necessary to withdraw the outposts altogether, falling back on the main position. Here the majority of the garrison would remain in cover without opening fire as long as possible, for premature fire within the main defended locality would allow enemy artillery and support weapons to identify and neutralise them. Machine guns which were called upon to fire at medium to long range were to do so from alternative positions, allowing them to move to their close defence positions later in the action without giving them away.

If the enemy penetrated the main position, every effort was to be made to destroy him by fire. If this failed, local counter-attacks were to be launched in short order, before the enemy had had a chance to gain a foothold and dig in. If faced by a tank attack, light machine guns and rifles were to take cover where they were, and not attempt to engage vehicles which they could not destroy. If, however, they had the chance to engage enemy infantry accompanying the tanks they should do so, with the objective of separating the tanks from their support. Armoured vehicles were to be fired on by anti-tank guns, and by anti-tank rifles, the latter joining in the fight when the enemy came within 300 metres. Where tanks had been isolated or immobilised the opportunity arose to attack and deal with them individually.

As far as enemy aircraft were concerned, it was usual to earmark at least the machine guns of one platoon to air defence, as it was not thought effective to devote less than three weapons to the task. Ideally the anti-aircraft group was placed about 300 metres from the troops to be protected, and an interval of fifty or sixty metres was allowed between weapons. The gun positions were then camouflaged in such a way that the branches or covers used could be swiftly removed. This deployment ensured that the anti-aircraft weapons could cover the sky above the potential target without giving away its precise location. The interval between machine guns allowed the guns to cover each other, without themselves creating a bunched target.

One commander was allotted to all three AA guns, his job being to remain with one of them, which then became the 'directing gun'. On the appearance of aircraft, the guns would begin to track the lowest lead machine, whether or not the planes had been identified as hostile. The gun commander would then attempt to establish the nationality of the aircraft, and when satisfied they were the enemy would order his gun to open fire. The other weapons would follow the lead of the directing gun. Whenever possible, all three machine guns would concentrate their fire on a single machine thus making it more difficult for the enemy to evade being hit. Rifle fire was also sometimes added to the AA cover, but again anything less than the use of a whole platoon, against the nearest

The heavy weapons company comes up in close support of the infantry attack. Note the *Unteroffizier* leading the section with P08 semi-automatic and stick grenade, and the various devices for holding helmet camouflage.
TRH Pictures

aircraft, was thought to be a waste of effort.

The keynotes to any defence were that it remain flexible; include provision for counterstrokes; bring to bear as much firepower as possible; and be concealed until the enemy was upon it. The idea was not to hold any particular feature all the time but to defeat the enemy, and eventually be able to control the desired terrain. It is interesting to note that in some instances these local precepts were applied to whole theatres of war. As Siegfied von Westphal said of the *Afrika Korps* in North Africa, the task was 'strategically defensive', but Rommel endeavoured to fulfil his task with 'timely tactical offensives'. It was a valuable lesson which was not always appreciated, particularly by those thinking in propaganda terms of square kilometres of territory held.

ASSAULT TROOPS AND ARMOUR

Whilst the organisation and small unit tactics of the infantry built directly on the experience of the Great War Stormtrooper, the Panzerschütze or Panzergrenadier marked a significant advance for which there was little obvious precedent prior to the inter-war period. In 1939, the armoured divisions which spearheaded the attack on Poland had contained a tank brigade consisting of two tank regiments, and a motorised infantry brigade of two regiments. This represented a mix of about 400 light and medium tanks with four battalions of mobile infantry. That winter however saw the formation of armoured divisions which had one tank regiment, containing only 200 mainly medium tanks, with four Panzergrenadier battalions. As Wilhelm Necker explained in the *German Army of Today*: 'The Germans, at an early stage of the war, and even before the war, understood the special weakness of the tank: its dependency on the terrain and the fact that it cannot occupy, but can only strike hard at and break through lines. For this reason the actual tank force was cut down to the very minimum and the division reinforced with

various other units, the most important of which is the Panzergrenadier regiment...' So it was that the assault troop content of the armoured division included not only the two *Panzergrenadier* regiments, but an armoured engineer battalion and an armoured reconnaissance battalion.

In the course of a set piece offensive of the early war period, the armoured spearhead attacked in co-ordination with artillery bombardment, aerial artillery in the shape of dive bombers, and assault engineers, with armoured or motorised infantry following close behind in order to enlarge the gaps cut by the armour. Ordinary infantry then surrounded, mopped up, and dealt with stubborn centres of resistance. As F.O. Miksche observed, writing in 1941, this was the old Stormtrooper 'infiltration' writ large: it was no longer a mere tactical method but a plan of strategic significance. The attack through France in particular would be a 'sickle cut', a passing through which caused the collapse of the enemy, rather than an attempt to take a specific position. Remarkably the actual Schwerpunkt, or focus of the attack, was often on a very narrow front. An attack front might be as little as a dozen miles; and within this the critical enemy positions might cover only a fraction of the ground. Miksche christened the resultant breakthrough a motorised 'irruption'.

This was a very different matter to the comparatively wide battlefronts tackled by the Stormtroopers of old, yet there were unmistakable similarities in concept, and the *Panzergrenadier* could be equally daring, as Guderian recorded during the attack on the French forts around Belfort in 1940: 'The tactics employed were very simple; first a short bombardment by the artillery... then Eckinger's rifle battalion, in armoured troop carrying vehicles, and an 88 mm AA gun drove right up to the fort, the latter taking up position immediately in front of the gorge; the riflemen thus reached the glacis without suffering any casualties and climbed up it, clambered over the entrenchments and scaled the wall while the 88 mm... fired into the gorge at point blank range. The fort was then summoned to surrender, which under the impact of the rapid attack, it did... our assault troops turned to their next task. Our casualties were very light.'

During the attack on Russia, however, the basic armoured assault troop precept underwent modifications, dictated at least in part by the relatively open and vast terrain, a small taste of which had already been glimpsed through campaigning in North Africa. The changes also attempted to take into account both Russian organisational improvements after the initial shock

of operation *Barbarossa*, and the fact that the enemy was learning tactically how to separate attacking tanks from infantry. As anti-tank defences improved it often became necessary to precede the tanks with engineers or lorried infantry, or with a mixed force of tanks and troops to clear obstacles and anti-tank teams.

Thus it was that from 1941 onwards, tanks and their assault infantry worked in even closer co-ordination. One of the key formations was the *Pulk*, a typically German contraction of *Panzer und Lastkraftwagen*, meaning literally 'tanks and trucks'. The *Pulk* was a hollow wedge or quadrangle of

Officers observe the action from an Sd Kfz 251 half track before Novgorod, 23 August 1941. *TRH Pictures*

tanks, inside which moved the column of motorised transport. The point was formed by the strongest tanks, and the sides by tanks and motorised guns. The wedge pierced the enemy defence line, its shape naturally widening the gap as it passed through. The motorised infantry were thus assisted to penetrate the defensive zone, and to spread out taking on any remaining resistance from the flanks and rear. Where the weakest point in the enemy line had not been definitely identified, the *Pulk* could advance as a blunt open backed quadrangle rather than a point. Once the route of least resistance was found, the whole formation could incline left or right, the corner of the quadrangle becoming a point in its own right. The disadvantage of the *Pulk* could be that its speed was limited to that of the slowest tank, and that for at least a short time vulnerability to enemy bombardment was increased. Despite the risks, troops were often actually carried into action on the tanks, debussing as a British intelligence document observed, 'at the last possible moment, using mainly light automatic weapons'.

Training for the *Panzergrenadiers* emphasised not only close co-operation with the tanks, but the natural strengths of armoured infantry: speed, cross country mobility, high firepower, and, where mounted in armoured half tracks, protection against small arms. As the 1942 manual for *Schnellen Truppen* observed, the *Panzergrenadierkompanie* was suited to both tank-infantry and independent operations. This could involve taking and holding ground already won by the tanks, or seeking out nests unidentified, or inaccessible to, the armour. Recent training based on Eastern Front experience also emphasised the potential need for long distance foot marches day or night, radio communications, and survival and efficiency in low temperatures.

PANZERGRENADIER TACTICS

The basic *Panzergrenadier* unit was the *Gruppe*, or squad, nominally totalling 12 personnel mounted in an armoured half-track; or, where this was unavailable, a truck. The men of the squad were the *Gruppenführer* and his assistant; two light machine gun teams, each of two men; four *Schützen* or riflemen; the driver or *Fahrer*, and his assistant or *Beifahrer*. As the *Militärwochenblatt* explained in September 1942, the *Schütze* of the Panzer infantry was rechristened *Grenadier*. This was due to his specialist status, and his similarity to the grenadiers of old who traditionally fought in advance of the unit. Though new, the armoured infantry were thereby rooted in the Stormtroop tradition. A *Panzergrenadier* platoon was made up of three squads, plus the platoon headquarters in a

separate vehicle. This headquarters or *Zugtrupp* consisted of the platoon commander; a driver; a radio operator; two messengers; a motorcycle messenger; a medic; and very often some form of anti-tank weapon such as a 37 mm gun mounted on the vehicle, and, or, an anti-tank rifle.

The impressive armament of the *Panzergrenadier* section from the middle period of the war was two, preferably three, light machine guns; two machine pistols; six rifles; four pistols; a rifle grenade launcher; hand and smoke grenades, and shaped charges. The squad leader or *Gruppenführer*, usually armed with a machine pistol, with torch, whistle, and wire cutters to hand, led the squad and was responsible to the platoon commander for both men and equipment. On the move he acted as vehicle commander, and fired the vehicle mounted machine gun. His deputy or *Truppführer* carried a rifle and spare ammunition, and could lead one part of the squad if divided. The Nr 1 in each machine gun team actually fired the machine guns, and thus led the fire fight when dismounted; when travelling in the vehicle one weapon was usually devoted to air defence. The second man in each machine gun team carried ammunition, assisted the gunners, and was commonly deployed a little to the left or behind the machine gunner in action. The four riflemen were the essential close combat component of the squad, and could engage any target with fire, but could also shoot from the vehicle if it was close assaulted. The driver not only drove the vehicle but was responsible for its care and camouflage and though he was expected to remain with the transport he was also rifle armed. The driver's assistant similarly remained with the vehicle, operating the radio, machine gun or machine pistol as required.

The text book method of mounting the vehicle was from the rear. On the command *Aufsitzen!*, the men climbed in, passing the weapons to avoid damage, with the *Truppführer* responsible for securing the door. Ideally, the squad leader sat towards the front, his assistant at the rear, and the men rearranged their gas masks onto their chest or stomach for comfort. In an armoured half track the driver and co-driver's hatches could be closed or opened on the command *Luken dicht!* or *Luken auf!* On the move it was usual for a man to be appointed for air observation, and one or more for observation to the sides. If the enemy was near the squad leader would keep smoke grenades handy to provide a screen, and on the command *Gefechtsbereitschaft!* the whole team would ensure they were loaded and ready.

Where a platoon was driving together, close order for convoy was understood to be five to ten

Next page, Squad attack through a Russian village, riflemen and sub-machine gunners moving at the double. *TRH Pictures*

metres apart, one behind the other, or even abreast in open country. In action, gaps between vehicles were extended upwards of 50 metres, and where possible ragged lines or chequer formations were preferred, reducing the chances of being hit and maximising opportunity. If a whole battalion deployed, this was often into an arrowhead. Troop carrying half tracks did not usually drive very fast, with even trucks calculating on an average of less than 30 km per hour road speed. Even under ideal circumstances the armoured division was not expected to cover more than 200 km in a 24 hour period. Remarkably, *Panzergrenadiers* were sometimes expected to advance in front of tanks, mounted or on foot, and supported by assault engineers. This was particularly the case in built up areas.

Communication between individual mobile sections could be done by messenger, lights, flags, or discs, but there was also a system of simple arm signals. The most important of these were a crank like motion for starting engines; bringing the arm down suddenly for halt or dismount; rapidly moving the arms outward from the chest to give the warning to take cover; and repeatedly pushing out one arm to give a movement direction. Loading or unloading equipment was signalled by swinging an arm in front of the body.

In armoured half tracks, drivers were prepared simply to drive through small arms fire, but would attempt to evade artillery or mortar fire. The machine gunners would attempt to engage targets on the move, and where the vehicle actually overran an enemy position, grenades were to be thrown and rifles and machine pistols used from the sides. Running the enemy over was by no means excluded. Under favourable circumstances one or more half tracks could indulge in a motorised version of fire and movement, shooting, driving and stopping so as to take advantage of cover. The squad leader could direct the fire or attention of his men to different targets by the clock face system; thus an enemy at 12 *Uhr* was directly to the front, and at 6 *Uhr* directly to the rear. The vehicle could halt to give a steady fire platform, but was recognised to be vulnerable if it did so. As a result it was not usual to halt in hostile open terrain for more than 15 to 25 seconds.

The normal dismount reversed the loading procedure, but in emergency the command *Abspringen!* was given, resulting in all parties jumping over the sides as well as out of the back ready for action. It was expected that the emergency exit could be performed even with the vehicle moving at slow speeds. Dismounted, the *Panzergrenadier* fought in a similar way to the infantry in ragged *Kette* and *Reihe* formations, except that usually having two machine guns these could be put either at the heads of the subsections or placed towards the centre.

DRIVE TO THE EAST

The attacks in Poland, Scandinavia, and the West had had their moments of difficulty, but hitherto every effort had been crowned by victory. Though large countries, neither France nor Poland were limitless in space, nor were their armies individually capable of outnumbering the German invasion forces. In the Soviet Union it would be otherwise. In June 1941, three million German soldiers faced five million Russians, and behind them a nation of 170 million people capable of fielding apparently endless reserves and absorbing incredible hardship. Herculean industrial efforts would ultimately enable Soviet production of 12,000 tanks and 20,000 aircraft per year. Moreover, the terrain of 'Mother Russia' was vast, and varied from open steppe to forest and marsh. Nevertheless, the first onslaught of Operation Barbarossa was impressive: vast *Kiel und Kessel* or 'wedge and cauldron' battles of encirclement isolated pockets the size of small countries which yielded the better part of two million prisoners. On a tactical level the Soviet army had been caught in the process of reorganisation under Defence Commissar Timoshenko's reforms. The faults of tight formations and lack of light machine guns so cruelly exposed in battle against the Finns had yet to be fully corrected, but space, German over-confidence, and the willingness of the Russian infantry to take casualties bought time.

Ideally, Soviet infantry were organised into nine man rifle sections based around light machine guns, with one of the regimental support companies entirely sub-machine gun armed. Yet especially in the early part of the war, Russian small unit tactics were often unsophisticated, with rifle companies being thrown forward in lines, wedges, and reverse wedges. Many of the new and only partially trained Militia or *opolchentsy* divisions were as yet incapable of anything else. As German observers at Zelva noted soon after the invasion: 'Again and again they swept up against the German positions with their unnerving cries of "*Urra!*" – companies, battalions, regiments. The picture was one that made the German troops' imagination boggle. The Russians were charging on a broad front, in an almost endless – seemingly solid line, their arms linked. Behind them a second, a third, and a fourth line abreast.'

Another German soldier faced with the same sort of attack, in which whole waves were shot down, described it as 'uncanny', 'unbelievable', even inhuman. Soon, however, the Russians were learning to be more circumspect. Rather than charge baldly from long range they would attempt to crawl close under cover of night or weather, and then rush in. Sometimes they adopted a strategy of infiltration, attempting to pass through thinly held German lines at night, and then attacking from all directions. By the end of 1941, a quarter of a million German soldiers were dead, significantly more than all the campaigns of 1939 and 1940 put together, and given the weather things were set to get worse. Operation *Typhoon* would grind to a halt before Moscow.

A roadside halt during the invasion of Russia, 1941. A man in the centre is wearing the motorcyclist's coat or Kradmantel. His gas mask case, or *Tragbüsche für Gasmaske*, has the anti-gas sheet attached and is worn on the front of the body, a more convenient position when seated or driving.
IWM HU 8895

END OF THE STORMTROOPER

Lack of a quick solution in the East cruelly exposed the failings of German military systems. Short term tactical elegance was not backed by long term strategy and the economy of the Fatherland was by no means geared to total war. Conditions on the Eastern Front were often such as to defy belief, especially in winter. Vehicles froze and refused to start unless kept warm by tins of burning fuel placed dangerously under their engines. The army slid rather than marched forward, whilst the Russians, who knew exactly what to expect, opened what they called 'winter roads', wide cross country tracts of compacted snow. Next fuel ran short; then ammunition, and clothes.

The Eastern Front medal would soon be wryly dubbed 'the Order of the Frozen Meat'. As Alexander Stahlberg recalled of the front near Leningrad, cold sapped morale as well as strength: 'Frost bitten limbs, feet, hands, ears, noses, mounted from day to day, but it was the wounded who were in the greatest danger. If frost penetrated an open wound it was unlikely the man could be saved. The men preferred death to injury. Doubts were beginning to gnaw at us all, from private soldier to Commanding Officer, but ultimately, we thought, 'them up there' must have recognised the mistakes made by the leadership and would avoid them in the future'. One of Stahlberg's colleagues was an officer called Englehardt, a Baltic German all too familiar with the ravages of Russian winter. As no warm clothes had arrived, Englehardt, like many others, set out to loot a winter wardrobe, and appeared attired in a huge civilian fur hat, and felt over boots lacking their soles. In Germany itself dire necessity would be turned to propaganda advantage with public collections of funds and often unsuitable clothing.

In the Spanish Blue Division, the men were particularly ill prepared for cold and men swapped weapons for fuel or clothes. Yet it seemed that supplies of winter uniform were not so much non-existent as inadequate and poorly distributed, with some divisions well equipped whilst many others made do with their great coats draped with white cotton bed sheets. Helmut Pabst would hear his outfit referred to as the 'Hunger Division', and see the men resort to Russian shirts and trousers as their own wore out. Yet even in his unit, fur caps, ear muffs, and quilted trousers were obtained for the most exposed, who also bound the outsides of their boots with rags to stave off frost. Men of the *Leibstandarte* hesitated to don enemy clothing for fear of accidents, but many were convinced by the cold and as a sop to uniformity, changed the Soviet star on the fur caps to death's heads.

The cold could cause some strange tactical problems. Infantry tended to hang close to the warmth of villages. This led to wide gaps in the lines, and to Soviet incursions. Frozen ground was difficult to dig, but parapets could be built of snow reinforced with wood. This would stop small arms, but only gave a false sense of security with shells. Wooden buildings were easy to loophole, but were vulnerable and the height of loopholes had to be judged according to the depth of the snow. Deep snow hindered mobility, and put a premium on vehicles with wide tracks. Snow could also mask anti-tank guns and assault guns, yet leave tanks whose turrets appeared above the snow line able to operate. General Otto Schellert of 253rd Infantry Division was intrigued to discover that machine guns would still work well below zero, but only if they were not oiled.

On a much more basic level, the worst cold of the open steppes made men aware that to shed any garments would result in frostbite; some just accepted the inevitable and were forced to defecate in their trousers. Eventually this problem was partially solved by making German army trousers accept belts; with no braces men stood a better chance of attending the urgent calls of nature without either freezing or being taken by surprise. The enemy faced the same sort of discomforts, yet they were more accustomed to the

weather and had more men to spare.

In spring the relief of warmer weather was of dubious benefit because the thaw brought with it the *rasputitsa*, the period when roads disappeared into mud slowing the advance and cutting off supplies. As von Thoma noted there never seemed to be enough half tracks, lorries were particularly prone to bogging down and 'only armoured infantry' could come into action quickly enough. The commander of Sixteenth Army's II Corps reported that rainy weather produced mud to the knees, caused fox holes to collapse, and the troops were reduced to eating cold food. His tip for 'limited' mobility was the use of Panje-wagons, light Russian horse drawn carts.

The war also took on an ideological dimension. Where the fight against the Western Allies was old fashioned in that it was about issues like territorial integrity and righting perceived historical wrongs; the war in the east was a clash of diametrically opposed political systems. Field Marshal von Reichenau explicitly stated in operational orders that the objective was to end the 'Jewish-Asiatic' danger. The *Ostfront* was soon painted not only as a *Rassenkampf* or 'race war' but as a war of national survival, Hitler describing it as a war of 'annihilation'. This it would become all too literally. Even for those who professed themselves

Official photograph showing Waffen SS combat troops wearing camouflage smocks and helmet covers clearing a village on the Eastern Front. The squad leader, left, is armed with the MP 40. Note the distinctive rune patches; rank was indicated by a system of pips and bars worn on the other wing of the collar.
TRH Pictures

apolitical, and opposed to the exterminations which went on around them, this was a war with a difference. Whole villages were burnt and cleared without concern for a population which alternately froze and starved. As Siegfried Knappe observed, one atrocity bred another, and when the infantry were fired on from behind as so often happened: 'Our soldiers went berserk, and from that point on during the attack they took no prisoners and left no one alive in a trench or a foxhole. I did not try to stop them, nor did any other officer because they would have killed us too if we had. They were out of their minds with fury.' Such things were all too common. As the history of the *Großdeutschland* division would put it, the battle became 'primeval', and man was transformed into 'an animal', who destroyed in order to live.

On the other side of the coin, these same men, who shared combat, 'became brothers, and this brotherhood is so important to them that they would give their lives for one another. It is not just friendship, and it is stronger than flag and country'. For Helmut Pabst the hardened combat veterans were survivors, almost a breed apart: 'who prowl through the countryside with slung rifles, jackets unbuttoned and caps askew. They have a look in their eyes which make them different from the rest. You know them immediately. They're the ones who carry on the war. They're indestructible. They drift around, game for anything. Danger attracts them, they love brushing with death. It's rare that such a man is caught. He's too quick, too skilful, too resolute. He masters the game and plays it for a long time. Then he breaks the rules once too often and meets his match. There was a Sergeant Major who had knocked out twenty-eight tanks in close combat; then he walked up to the commander of the twenty ninth with only his pistol in his hand... Such men are often difficult to handle in back areas, but at the front, if rightly handled by the right officer, they can turn a company into a first-rate fighting unit because their bold resolution transfers itself to all the rest. Courage is infectious just like cowardice.' Men like these contrasted sharply with newcomers, marked out by their new clothes, 'clean and free from lice, dignified and full of innocent intentions'.

Weather and Russian counter-attacks between them added up to a considerable attrition rate. By late 1941, the 142 divisions in the East were down to an average of a little over 50 percent of their original strength. In early 1942, six divisions totalling 96,000 men were cut off in the Demyansk pocket, just under half became casualties. The plight of individual units was often no less serious, and in this respect 12th Panzer Division was by no means unusual. Their war diary records that they numbered 13,976 men in December 1941, seven months later they were reduced to 3,229, and due to lack of vehicle detachments, were acting as infantry, fire fighting to cover gaps. At one point, just before Christmas 1941, 6th Panzer Division had no tanks left at all. In October 1941, the SS *Leibstandarte* submitted returns that showed its rifle companies averaged 66 men, or almost exactly a third of their official establishment. The elite *Großdeutschland* had a complete company wiped out in a forest ambush, and then lost heavily in repeated battles around Briansk and Tula. In November 1942, a complete battalion was

Greatcoated infantry make progress the hard way on the Eastern Front. Note the snow camouflaged steel helmets and the *StuG* III assault gun.

destroyed. Not long afterwards one of its companies' fighting strength was five men led by a Gefreiter, or lance corporal. 12th Infantry Division was a third of its theoretical strength by early 1943 and one of its 'battalions' reported with 46 men.

'Field replacement' units of the *Ersatzheer* were pushed straight into the line to make up shortfalls, and constant streams of conscripts were in demand. Yet it rarely proved possible to distribute replacements evenly or make up the numbers quickly enough at precisely the point they were needed. The result was a wide disparity in strength from unit to unit. In Model's Ninth Army in the spring of 1942, for example, the 206th Infantry Division boasted a respectable nine battalions of 8,100 men whilst 253rd Infantry had a mere three battalions with 3,400 men. At about the same time there were further reductions in the establishment of Panzer divisions, so that they could have anything between one and three battalions of *Panzergrenadier*.

Germany might still have been winning the war in an abstract sense, but as one general observed there was a danger that it might be 'destroyed by winning'. Yet the individual soldier continued to fight tenaciously. Ideology may have played a part, but equally important was the will to avoid capture. Draconian discipline must similarly have been a factor. During the course of the Second World War

about 14,000 German soldiers would be executed by their own side, the Kaiser's army had put to death but 48.

German Army intelligence soon speculated that the war in the East would not be won unless it could be turned into a civil war. To find more men the German army became progressively, what Field Marshal von Rundstedt would contemptuously call, a 'League of Nations' force. Complete armies of Rumanians, Italians and Hungarians were entrusted with vital parts of the line. Then the *Wehrmacht* accepted men who were, more or less, volunteers from outside Germany. The *Waffen* SS recruited first ethnic Germans, then Germanic troops of the 'correct' racial origins, then foreigners, then pretty well anyone. Still there were not enough men.

In many ways typical was the experience of Ukrainian Michael Paziuk, volunteer in theory perhaps, but actually guarded on his way to the selection centre. Here he would be medically examined, packed into an ill fitting cadet uniform and entrained for Czechoslovakia. Basic training was conducted in Austria and lasted about three months, was given in both his own language and German, and would include not only battle craft but drill, physical sports and route marches with singing.

Yet even whilst Ukrainians and Baltics were being raised, and Russians and Soviet minorities were being pressed as *Hilfswillige* or *Hiwi* auxiliaries, and Cossack divisions were formed, their countrymen were being starved, murdered, brutalised, or simply vilified as *Untermensch*. Both in word and deed the goodwill that many local populations had initially exhibited for their 'liberators' from Communism was undone and with time, desperation, and familiarity with death things would only get worse. Simply to get enough food to live often meant resisting the invader or cooperating with the partizans. To put it cynically, atrocity was often counter productive, but very few, like Generals Blaskowitz or Lemelsen, were brave

Convalescent soldiers, May 1942. Though a serious set-back had been experienced before Moscow, losses were still sustainable up until this time. After Stalingrad and the totalisation of the war it would be otherwise. By 1945 Germany would have 3.5 million military and two million civilian dead. *SB*

or stupid enough to point this out. News of the slaughters perpetrated in the East had even reached Paris by the end of 1942. Here Hauptmann Ernst Jünger, himself no stranger to death and brutality, confided to his diary that he was, 'seized with loathing for the uniforms, epaulets, medals and weapons whose splendour I have loved so.'

Though the Soviet army was cosmopolitan in its make-up and often patchy in its competence, close combat was its metier. If its tanks and artillery were deployed in copious amounts, then infantry was still regarded as the *Tsarita* of the battlefield to whom the actions of the other arms were geared. The Red Army was therefore adept at fighting in the close country of swamp and forest which the armoured thrusts of the Panzer divisions naturally tended to avoid. Where lightning attacks in the West had left isolated Allied units nowhere to hide, the vastness of the East and the size of the forests meant that encircled positions could often hold out for a considerable time, whilst German numbers were insufficient to complete what was theoretically a victory.

Where tanks and heavy weapons were at a loss, older methods were revived. Such was the case with *Kavallerie Brigade Model*, formed in the summer of 1942 to deal with a large body of the enemy who had broken through and formed a dangerous lodgement in swamps and forests to the rear of Ninth Army. Commanded by Colonel Karl-Friedrich von der Merden this consisted of three cavalry regiments of experienced Eastern Front fighters, half mounted on horses, half riding bicycles, armed mainly with machine weapons. A two-week campaign wiped out the threat. Nor was this the only form of unconventional warfare as *Obersturmführer* Eric Brörup, fighting as a platoon commander with a ski reconnaissance unit of the SS Viking division, would report: 'Fighting in trees is a little different from a traditional battle, where you usually have all kinds of fireworks – artillery,

mortars, rockets, machine guns – and all kinds of other hardware to back you up. In the trees you are on your own. The weapons we used for forest fighting were just rifles, machine pistols and grenades. It is also very sneaky. You work in circles around each other in a kind of deadly "hide and seek".'

Yet the Germans had no monopoly on ruthlessness, and were by no means guaranteed success. Partizans could be as lethal as the men who tried to hunt them, and the Russians had no scruple about augmenting their combat strength even further by recruiting women for front line units. The NKVD were prone to punish any who showed

Cautious support for a machine gun team during street fighting, Stalingrad 1942. One of the troops in the foreground carries a spare barrel and machine gun ammunition.
TRH Pictures

even the slightest lack of enthusiasm, and others at random for good measure. The commander of the wavering 64th Soviet rifle division probably did his men a favour by shooting some of them personally rather than letting things become 'official'. On at least one occasion the Russians were observed to clear a mine field by the simple expedient of having a punishment battalion march through it in close order. *Sturmbahnführer* Kurt Meyer recorded that within weeks of the opening of the campaign the murder of prisoners was occurring; and described finding a complete company bound and shot by the Soviets.

The advice given to the German *Landser*

departing for the *Ostfront* similarly gave a chilling hint of what was in store for him: 'The soldier in Russia must be a hunter. The Bolshevist's greatest advantage over the German is his highly developed instinct and his lack of sensitivity to the weather and to the terrain. One must be able to walk and creep like a huntsman. The soldier in Russia must be able to improvise: the Bolshevist is a master of improvisation. The soldier in Russia must constantly be on the move. Hardly a day passes on which the Russians, however weak they may be, do not attempt to push against our lines. Day after day they work to improve their positions. The soldier in Russia must be suspicious. The soldier in Russia

Squad leaders receive orders during the battle for Stalingrad. Note the camouflaged helmet cover and the captured SVT 40 semi-automatic rifle of the man nearest the camera.
IWM HU 5149

must be wide awake. The Russian practically always attacks during the night and in foggy weather. In the front line there is nothing to be done but to remain awake at night and rest during the day. But in Russia there is no front line or hinterland... Anyone who lays down his arms east of the old Reich frontier may greatly regret this a moment later... The soldier in Russia must be hard. Real men are needed to make war in 40 degrees of frost or in great heat, in knee deep mud or in thick dust. The victims of Bolshevist mass attacks often present a sight against which the young soldier must harden his heart.'

If Moscow and Leningrad halted the advance, then it was Stalingrad which turned the war into a battle of attrition which had many of the hallmarks of the Great War, the war which had created many of the assault tactics which now strained to make little headway against a questionable strategic target. Not for nothing would Stalingrad be christened a 'Verdun on the Volga', and similarly many of the methods which were now used against the German infantry were essentially those defensive methods which the Imperial German Army had helped to develop.

The Russians usually relied on a defensive network of strong points rather than a line, and successful counter attacks were often the product of surprise rather than bombardment. Sometimes in built-up areas, the Russians would allow German troops and tanks to pass their strong points, which acted like breakwaters in a tide, and then open fire from the side or rear. When well fought, this was not street fighting – but building fighting – since those who showed themselves on the streets and squares were usually the first to die. German soldiers would christen this the *Rattenkrieg*, a veritable war of rats in which men fought through cellars and sewers as well as buildings. Small assault squads of half a dozen would go armed with knives and entrenching tools as well as grenades and sub-machine guns, and prise out the

opposition. Pioneers with flamethrowers and explosive charges could give a considerable edge in confined spaces. The Russians also had their own vocabulary for this vicious war within a war: the fighters referred to themselves as being trained in the 'Stalingrad Academy of Street Fighting'; grenades became 'gherkins'; bullets, 'sunflower seeds'.

The Soviets showed an almost unbelievable tenacity. In perhaps the most celebrated example of fortitude, not to say pigheadedness, Sergeant Jacob Pavlov of the 13th Guards Division crammed 60 men plus support and anti-tank weapons into a single four-storey building and surrounded it with mines. German infantry and tanks were repelled, and it took 58 days to smash 'Pavlov's House' with bombing and artillery. Yet the best defence was, as always, elastic and mixed with counter strokes. As Soviet General Chuikov would observe: 'Experience showed that the 'storm groups' and the strong points were the most important facets of our defence. The army beat off enemy attacks, itself attacked, and made bold sallies, and took the initiative out of the enemy's hands. The power of our troops lay in the fact that, while defending themselves they attacked the whole time'.

It is interesting to observe that later on the German Sixth Army war diary similarly made

Action in the Ukraine. Infantry in padded winter combat dress accompanied by a *Schwimmwagen* amphibious car pass a burning Russian tank.
TRH Pictures

frequent mentions of 'enemy storm troop activity', and it was only with extreme difficulty that the Russian infantry assaults in the wake of Operation Uranus were temporarily held off. One of the most vivid accounts was left by Hans Urban, serving with the Hessian 389th Infantry Division at Christmas 1942: 'The enemy used to attack at dawn and dusk, after heavy artillery and mortar preparation. If they captured two or three bunkers from us, we would try and get them back later. On 30 December, after many of these attacks, I was ordered to take my rapid fire group forward. My nine men with their machine guns were able to hold off the next attack by about 300 men from Spartakova. The twenty infantrymen on this sector were so exhausted from all the attacks that they could not offer much help. Most were ready to abandon their positions. I had with my two machine guns no field of fire. The enemy were able to make use of the terrain and the ruins. We had to let the Russians get within twenty yards before opening rapid fire. At least 22 were left dead in front of our positions. The surviving Russians tried to flush us out with grenades. The Russians attacked again on the same sector at daybreak on New Year's morning with three companies. It's hard to make an accurate estimate because they were shooting from holes in the ground, from behind collapsed walls or piles of rubble. We got them in a cross fire from the two machine guns and they suffered heavy casualties... we were so weak and exhausted and there were so many dead lying around in the open frozen stiff, that we could not even bury our own comrades.'

In such warfare, sniping skills were at a premium, and in the absence of news of a victory the propagandists of both sides hyped up the tally of sudden death, and snipers became the stars of Stalingrad and other urban battlegrounds. On the Soviet side the most celebrated was Vasili Zaitzev, a hunter credited with more than a hundred kills in the autumn of 1942. Amongst others he claimed to have shot Major Konings, chief instructor of the German sniper school at Zossen, in a particularly stealthy duel: 'For a long time I examined the enemy positions, but could not detect his hiding place. From the speed with which he had fired, I came to the conclusion that the sniper was somewhere directly ahead of us. I continued to watch... Between the tank and the pillbox, on a stretch of level ground, lay a small pile of broken bricks. It had been lying there a long time and we had grown accustomed to it being there. I put myself in the enemy's position and thought – where better for a sniper ? One had only to make a firing slit under the sheet of metal, and then creep up to it during the night.

'Yes, he was certainly there, under the sheet of

Opposite, Anti-tank action Eastern Front 1944. Hand held anti-tank weapons became increasingly vital in the struggle against Soviet armour. The textbook defensive scheme was a system of anti-tank nests about 150m apart, two deep, and staggered, so that enemy tanks attempting to traverse the position would inevitably expose their vulnerable flanks or rear within a range of 75 metres. When confronted head on by the well armoured T 34, anti-tank teams were taught to aim for the driver or machine gunner's positions or the tracks.

The man foreground left is firing the *Raketenpanzerbüchse 54*: this 88mm rocket weapon weighed 11 kg, and had an armour piercing capability of 160 mm, at up to 180 metres. In *Panzergrenadier* units the projectors could be transported in racks on the half tracks, but infantry were usually limited to the use of a horse drawn cart on which six weapons were carried. The operator shown here is wearing the reversible padded jacket to the *Wintertarnanzug*, or winter camouflaged suit, over his basic uniform. The helmet cover is also in splinter pattern material, and has loops for the attachment of foliage. There were matching trousers to this outfit, but this man has omitted them and wears only the 1943 type field grey trousers with gaiters and ankle boots. His belt equipment includes a water bottle and ammunition carriers for the *Gewehr 43* semi-automatic rifle seen nearby. The pouches shown would contain a total of 40 rounds in four magazines: sometimes one G43 pouch was worn with a standard triple pouch on the other side of the belt.

The *Gefreiter* (lance-corporal) acting as loader for the *Raketenpanzerbüchse* is carrying a partially full five round wooden back pack for the missiles. Each hollow charge rocket round weighed 3.25 kg and the ammunition was produced in summer and winter varieties to take account of extremes of temperature. The loader stands well to the side of the *Raketenpanzerbüchse* to avoid back blast. This man is wearing the great coat, helmet with net, and gas mask case. Above his rank chevron is the Kuban shield, instituted in September 1943 for the defence of the Kuban bridgehead, following the debacle at Stalingrad. Recipients of the various arm shields were usually provided with more than one example of the award to be used on different orders of dress.

The Grenadier top left is aiming the *Panzerfaust 60*; a single shot weapon weighing 6.5 kg. This model could penetrate up to 240 mm of armour at a maximum of 80 metres: users were supposed to stay 30 metres from the target. The 150mm hollow charge projectile was immensely destructive, but relatively slow moving as it was shot from the launcher by a black powder charge. According to German statistics of April 1944, a total of 172 Russian vehicles fell victim to close combat in that month alone of which almost exactly two thirds were knocked out by the *Panzerfaust*. The veteran shown already has two enemy armoured fighting vehicles to his credit, as may be determined by the badges worn on the right upper arm of his *Feldbluse*.

Other things scattered around the position include four *Panzerfaust* in their wooden transport crate, and a 7.62 mm Soviet PPsh 41 sub-machine gun with its distinctive 71 round drum magazine: in German sevice this gun was known as the *Maschinenpistole 717 (r)*. So many of these were captured that some were even converted to accept 9 mm ammunition and box magazines. The 20 litre jerry can with a smoke grenade tied to it is a makeshift weapon of last resort: the grenade would be activated and the whole contraption hurled bodily against the tank.
Painting by Richard Hook

metal in no man's land. I thought I would make sure. I put a mitten on the end of a small plank and raised it. The Nazi fell for it. I carefully let the plank down in the same position as I had raised it and examined the bullet hole. It had gone straight through from the front; that meant that the Nazi was under the sheet of metal. Now came the question of luring even a part of his head into my sights... We worked by night and were in position by dawn. The sun rose. Kulikov took a blind shot ; we had to rouse the sniper's curiosity. We had decided to spend the morning waiting, as we might have been given away by the sun on our telescopic sights. After lunch our rifles were in the shade and the sun was shining directly on the German's position... Kulikov carefully – as only the most experienced can do – began to raise his helmet. The German fired. For a fraction of a second Kulikov rose and screamed. The German believed that he had finally got the Soviet sniper he had been hunting for four days, and half raised his head from behind the sheet of metal. That was what I had been banking on. I took careful aim. The German's head fell back, and the telescopic sights of his rifle lay motionless...'

Though doubt has been cast on the specifics of this particular account, it is typical of many such incidents, and amongst the Soviets there would arise a veritable cult of 'sniperism' which was portrayed as 'socialistic competition' and rewarded with medals. Another famous protagonist was Kovbasa, a Ukrainian of 64th Army who specialised in working from a warren of interconnected trenches and dummy positions. His favourite trick was to raise a white flag and then shoot any who popped up to accept surrender.

Yet the sniper war was anything but one-sided. Amongst the Germans, Matthias Hetzenauer of 3rd Mountain Division would be credited with 345 kills, and acclaimed as the nation's top sniper. The same division also contained Sepp Allerberger with 257, and Helmut Wirnsberger with 64 enemy hit. All were what Hetzenauer would call 'tacticians of detail'. As in the First World War, sniper training took place behind the front, and men were taught to be cautious and reserve their fire. To these ends the maxim was 'camouflage ten times, shoot once'. In addition to camouflage clothing, hoods, veils, mats of grass, screens, nets and folding umbrella-like structures were all used to provide extra cover. In 1944 special sniper badges were introduced, though rarely displayed for obvious reasons. For the SS, Himmler even proposed a bizarre productivity scheme, by which 50 kills would be rewarded by a wrist watch, 100 a hunting rifle, and 150 a personal invitation to go on a hunting trip. In Normandy, German snipers were a veritable plague, crawling

Panzer destroyed in street fighting. The advent of powerful armour by no means spelt the end of assault infantry. *Panzergrenadiers* were required to escort the tanks which were at a dreadful disadvantage in confined spaces. *SB*

forward, up trees, and camouflaged in the hedges of the *bocage*. Allied officers hastily removed their distinguishing marks and began to carry rifles; further back even mortar and artillery crews had to take extra care.

Stalingrad saw the end of Sixth Army, the last starved remnants of which surrendered at the beginning of February 1943, but it did not see the end of offensives in the East. During Operation *Citadel* it was arguable that a greater and more damaging folly was committed, for at Kursk Hitler threw not only 2,000 tanks but 25 infantry divisions against the solid Russian line. Yet without surprise there could be no Blitzkrieg, and the Soviets were not only ready in greater numbers but in a *Pakfront* organised in depth. Kursk, therefore, deteriorated into a mechanised attrition in which the Germans gave as good as they got, but were systematically reduced until the Soviets themselves took the initiative and counter-attacked. Moreover, Russian minor tactics showed noticeable improvement. As a report filed by German Ninth Army in 1944 would relate, the Russians: 'no longer attacked, as in the past, on a broad front with a very heavy artillery support, but employed concentrated groups of infantry supported by tightly concentrated and well controlled fire from heavy weapons... behind these assault groups, undisclosed until needed, lay the tank forces...'

The great battles of 1942 to 1944 left an indelible impression. For Siegfried Knappe it was the sheer noise of the set piece action which was most impressive: 'The sound of combat was deafening. It was like combining every loud noise anyone ever heard into one colossal, deafening roar. It was a virtual hurricane of noise, but it does not pass by as a hurricane does; it remained as long as the fighting went on... The roar of combat alone was enough to shatter a soldier's will. But combat was a great deal more than just noise. It was a whirlwind of iron and lead that howled about the soldier, slicing through anything it hit. Even inside the roar of battle, strangely, the soldier could detect the whistle of bullets and the hum of slivers of shrapnel, perceiving everything separately – a shell burst here, the rattle of a machine gun over there... In spite of the confusion... the soldier... felt an almost palpable sense of solidarity with his fellow soldiers. This was the brotherhood of the combat soldier.'

For *SS Schütze Gührs* of the *Leibstandarte*, battle started as a ear splitting experience with assault guns and artillery booming, and machine gun bullets 'slashing' through foliage. Then, however, sound was then blotted out as the closest guns masked all noise. As he put it 'the whole experience had a primitive power and was in an

unreal way very beautiful'. Some of the worst incoming fire came from the truck mounted *Katyuska* ('Little Kate') rocket batteries, which the Germans dubbed the Stalin Organ. These were often massed for effect so that a *Katyuska* division was capable of launching 3840 projectiles in short order, thereby dumping 230 tons of high explosive on the target.

NEW WEAPONS AND TACTICS

The basics of German infantry combat may have seen few major changes in the latter part of the war, but new arms did bring with them a need for new techniques. Arguably the most important influences on minor tactics were the introduction of more effective hand held anti-tank weapons, and the continuing proliferation of light automatic and semi-automatic weapons. Though dangerous to use effectively the *Panzerfaust* and the magnetic mine would prove to be weapons which helped overcome the apparent powerlessness of infantry in the face of tanks.

Some idea of just what it took to engage in tank hunting with hand held weapons is provided by Guy Sajer's account of training with the *Großdeutschland* division: 'As we had already been taught to dig a foxhole in record time, we had no trouble opening a trench 150 metres long, half a metre wide, and a metre deep. We were ordered into the trench in close ranks, and forbidden to leave it no matter what happened. Then four or five Mark III [tanks] rolled forward at right angles to us and crossed the trench at different speeds. The weight of these machines alone made them sink five or ten centimetres into the crumbling ground. When their monstrous treads ploughed into the rim of the trench only a few centimetres from our heads, cries of terror broke... we were also taught how to handle the dangerous *Panzerfaust*, and how to attack tanks with magnetic mines. One had to hide in a hole and wait until the tank came close enough. Then one ran, and dropped an explosive device – unprimed during practice – between the body and the turret of the machine. We weren't allowed to leave our holes until the tank was within five metres of us. Then, with the speed of desperation, we had to run straight at the terrifying monster, grab the tow hook and pull ourselves onto the hood, place the mine... and drop off the tank to the right with a decisive rolling motion.'

Despite the best laid schemes it was seldom as smooth as this in practice. Many men were cut down by machine gun fire, or run over by their target. Miss fires sometimes occurred with the Panzerschreck rocket launcher, and also with the *Panzerfaust* as was recorded by SS

Obersturmführer Eric Brörup in action in Hungary: 'I got an SdKfz 250 / 9 and went into battle. We were firing high explosive shells and it seemed easy, like shooting fish in a barrel. Then the Russians brought up an anti-tank rifle and shot up my vehicle, forcing us to bail out. We ended up in hand-to-hand combat with them. I had a *Panzerfaust* anti tank rocket but it wouldn't fire. I therefore used it like a club and cracked one Russian's head with it. I was in trouble though... I got the Iron Cross First Class for all this.'

When they did work however, these apparently Heath Robinson contraptions could be devastating. Shaped charges had the effect of concentrating explosive blast onto a tiny spot; and some projectiles were so designed that a jet of molten metal was created at the epicentre of the explosion. In Normandy there would be accounts of Sherman tank turrets hit on one side by a concealed *Panzerfaust* operator, and so thoroughly penetrated that a hole would appear in the far side.

The result was that Allied aggression was modified by the very possibility that German anti-tank teams would be present. On one occasion late in the war, a squadron of 1st Royal Tank Regiment would be held up for hours by a small party of Germans behind a road block, justified hesitancy if there were no infantry on hand to deal with rocket teams. The history of British 7th Armoured Division recorded that its tanks took to spraying the sides of the roads with machine gun fire, or charging around at top speed to minimise the chance of being hit. Sometimes crews had the horrible feeling that it was a choice between staying in the vehicle and being hit with a *Panzerfaust*, or bailing out and being sniped. Like the Germans in Russia, the Western Allies learned to mix tanks with infantry; carry infantry on the tanks; or lead with the foot soldiers supported by tanks.

The proliferation of light automatic weapons likewise had its own tactical impacts. Fewer men had more to do, but being given new automatics like the MG 42 and the *Sturmgewehr*, and an increased allotment of the existing arms improved the chances of success. British troops received more than a taste in Normandy, as Major Cooke of the Royal Scots recalled: 'The men, their faces strained, speak in tired, low voices, almost fearful of breaking a spell... Over all of it runs the memory of an enemy who is seldom seen but often heard. As soon as darkness fell we could hear the crackle of a Spandau or the burrp-burrp of a machine pistol as the Boche once again began his night's work. During the day the crash of a sniper's rifle or the sudden mounting crescendo of mortar bombs, preceded by the unearthly groan of the rocket projector, caused dozing men to stare at each other

and bolt to their slit trenches... The Churchill tanks crawled up every morning to support the forward companies, and Boche snipers lay awaiting them ; their Bazookas... can pierce a Churchill turret at about 40 yards... The Boche showed individual determination and field craft of the highest order. The constant firing, now from the front, now from the flank, now from the rear... to draw answering fire and thus reveal our positions. At Estry I believe the enemy held their ground with the minimum of men and the maximum of weapons.'

On the *Ostfront* there was often a similarly profligate use of automatic fire; meeting attacks, or even potential attacks with walls of bullets. As one Russian account describing the use of German infantry put it: 'When advancing they did not spare their bullets but frequently fired into thin air. Their forward positions, particularly at night, were beautifully visible, being marked by machine gun fire, tracer bullets... and different coloured rockets'.

Also on the open battlefields of the East Helmut, Pabst observed the same phenomenon from a different perspective: 'On the whole war hasn't changed. Artillery and infantry still dominate the battlefield. The increased fire power of the infantry – automatic weapons, mortars and all the rest... but you have to accept the basic fact, you're after the other man's life. That's war. That's the trade. And it isn't so difficult. Again, because the weapons are automatic, most people don't realise the full implications of it: you kill from a distance, and kill people you don't know and don't see.'

Interestingly, the idea of using more automatic weapons and less men was officially reflected in the new organisational structure of the *Volksgrenadier* divisions raised in 1944. So it was that a *Volksgrenadier* battalion had roughly as many automatic weapons as rifles; and each company had two sub-machine gun platoons, each with a total of 29 automatic weapons, but only five rifles. In theory the infantry divisions raised in 1945 were to have fractionally more automatic weapons, and indeed Grenadier companies in which assault rifles were the main weapon.

DESPERATION

The last few months of war apparently saw the eclipse of the Stormtrooper as a decisive instrument of war, still relatively little changed in the basics of tactical thinking. As the American synthesis in the 1945 *Handbook on German Military Forces* observed: 'The fundamental principle of German offensive doctrine is to encircle and destroy the enemy. The objective of combined arms attack is to bring the armoured forces and the infantry into decisive action against the enemy with sufficient fire power and shock. Superiority in force and fire power, the employment of armoured forces, as well as the surprise element, play a great part in the offensive.'

Small counter attacks continued to play a significant part in defensive war. In the West, it was observed that minor ripostes, sometimes by platoons, could be expected immediately after Allied troops arrived on German positions. Advancing by fire and movement and making maximum use of automatic weapons they would attempt to drive the Allies out; often from a flank and usually by fire rather than the bayonet.

Yet in the face of political and strategic failure,

the prerequisites of tactical success were rarely to hand, or rarely made a decisive contribution to the strategic situation. As in the Great War, Germany was again fighting a two, or three front war, and despite the near miracles worked by Albert Speer, blockade and bombing were beginning to impinge upon supplies of vital resources. Superiority of force was no longer to hand. To make matters worse, the Allies had achieved air domination over the battlefield which severely limited movement. Opportunities for surprise were strictly limited: Allied intelligence was much improved, and Allied armies were now numerous, well armed, and wary. It was also arguable that when offensive action had

Ready to go over the top. Though lightly equipped the soldier nearest the camera carries the folding spade or *Klappspaten* and bayonet on his belt. Note also the various helmet camouflage and the light-weight *Tarnjacke* or camouflage smock.
TRH Pictures

been possible it had been misapplied. Where the great offensive drives of 1939 and 1940 had deliberately avoided built up areas like Paris, or fortifications such as the Maginot Line, later campaigns had become bogged down in Russian cities, or had fallen upon prepared defences, as at Kursk. 'Hold at all costs' orders were also too freely given where retreats mixed with local counter attacks might have led to greater success.

However, this did not mean that sections of assault troops with their personal weapons were redundant, as the American tacticians put it: 'At the present time, the offensive tactics of the Germans are less spectacularly bold than they were in 1939, but the fundamental theory behind them has changed very little... The Germans learned at heavy cost the futility of charging a hostile anti-tank defence... They have learned that large formations of tanks cannot achieve a breakthrough opposed by an effective screen of anti-tank guns, without the assistance of other arms. Therefore attention has to be given to the combined tactics of tanks and the *Panzergrenadiers...*'

It was also noticeable that this emphasis on combined arms, with limited resources, led to a *Kampfgruppe* approach, where the commander of a formation would have a selection of units – armour, infantry or artillery – added to his order of battle as necessary to the task in hand. If tanks were available, they would attack in two or three waves: one to crash through and neutralise the anti-tank defence and artillery, another following to take out infantry positions in close co-operation with *Panzergrenadiers*. Often the tanks and motorised infantry would themselves act by fire and movement, advancing and covering each other in bounds. When actually under fire, trained infantry would learn to stay clear of the immediate vicinity of the individual tanks since these acted as magnets for enemy fire.

Arguably the most famous *Kampfgruppe* action of all was that of Joachim Peiper's armoured spearhead during the Ardennes offensive, but though it was his *Königstiger* which has captured the popular imagination, his own accounts make it clear that the armour was useless when unsupported. Initially, half tracks were mixed with Panzers, and later parachute troops or *Panzergrenadiers* were carried into action on the tanks. Sometimes movement was confined to the hours of darkness and, according to one eyewitness account, when the going was bad and blackout conditions were required, the tanks had to be guided by parachutists who walked ahead holding white handkerchiefs. Near Stavelot a Panzer IV was mined and sloughed its track, thus

blocking the road. The initial attack was therefore dependent on a 'scratch force' of 60 *Panzergrenadiers* who were themselves halted by machine gun and artillery fire.

Physical features similarly tended to dictate the course of events, as at Petit-Spai where a bridge gave way under the weight of an assault gun. At other times, progress was decided by supplies, road blocks, or single anti-tank guns, and usually these problems had to be surmounted by engineers or infantry who cleared the way for the armour. Where the attack co-ordinated assault troops and tanks, as at Stoumont, the result was success. The message was clear: without determined assault troops even the most awesome armour was vulnerable. When Peiper's *Kampfgruppe* was finally defeated, it was not because of tank to tank action, but because American infantry and air power effectively cut off and immobilised the armour. Peiper's tanks were stranded, yet almost 800 men were still able to break out and escape on foot.

Occasionally tactical situations would dictate that infantry and engineer formations attack by themselves, or opening up the defensive line first to allow tank and motorised breakthrough. Such was often the case in the Ardennes where as Manteuffel put it, 'my Storm battalions infiltrated rapidly into the American front – like rain drops', to be followed only later by the tanks advancing under cover of night or bad weather to avoid the attentions of Allied air power. In such instances many of the old infantry assault tactics would again come to the fore, but with some added refinements. These might include attempts at infiltration hours, or even days, prior to the main assault, and brief bombardments by heavy guns which would not only discomfort the defence but pit the ground with shell holes to cover the attackers. Once *Stosstrupp* groups had achieved a lodgement, aided forward by anti-tank guns and flamethrowers, the infantry would then attempt to break out, rolling outwards from the point of penetration. This would preferably be covered by assault gun groups advancing immediately behind the infantry to neutralise enemy support weapons.

With fairly limited exceptions, such as the Ardennes, the last year of war was the story of dogged defence. According to the textbook, defence in depth was still the order of the day, with infantry weapons and anti-tank guns holding their fire until the attackers were easy targets, preferably with smoke fired into the midst of the enemy formation to hinder communication and silhouette the leading elements against the smoke. In towns and villages, the bulk of the defenders were to be held back from the edges, thereby avoiding the

Opposite, an MG 34 machine gun team on the Eastern Front. The MG 34 was arguably the first really successful 'general purpose' machine gun; working well as both a squad weapon from the bipod, or as seen here, in the sustained fire role from the steady platform of the *Maschinengewehr-Lafette 34*. Ranges up to 3500 metres were claimed.

worst of the enemy fire. Reserves should then have counteracted any breakthrough.

Such niceties were not always possible and the limited mobile units were forced to act as 'fire fighters' racing to plug gaps in the line. When tanks and armoured personnel carriers were exhausted, carts and hand held anti-tank weapons had to suffice. This was the sort of morale sapping experience described by teenage Ukrainian Michael Paziuk, near Zilina in Slovakia in January 1945. Where, after subsisting on an inadequate diet of watery potato and pea soup and half frozen black bread, he was finally ordered up to the front: '...after an hour of waiting, we were informed that there would be no train to take us, [and] we would have to walk like "sheep to the slaughter". Divided into three platoons, riflemen, mortar Grenadiers and machine gunners (I belonged to the latter), we were given permission to find some wood that would be suitable for making sledges to transport the ammunition. We found a couple of hammers and some nails in a work shed and began to dismantle the station fence... we made the sledge large enough to carry the ammunition and the two rifles of the lads who would be pulling. We also took our turn to carry the machine gun, which after a time became very heavy and very uncomfortable as it began to dig into the shoulder... The walk itself (which lasted about six days) nearly killed me.'

Neither were such exertions rewarded with success. Even before Paziuk's unit had deployed from the march it came under sniper fire, losing its sergeant. The action then dissolved into a confused fire fight: 'One of the groups ran towards the bank and were immediately engaged in firing their weapons. Our group, now without its Sergeant, moved up the bank further on and I, carrying two big cases of ammunition, followed the machine gunner. We were just about to set up the machine gun in position when mortar bombs started dropping all around us. Splinters whined through the air cutting men down all about me. Some screamed in agony, others died silently. Andrey, the machine gunner was hit in the leg and disappeared behind the bank'. Paziuk was also wounded. His first taste of action had taken eight months of preparation and lasted no more than minutes.

On many occasions, terrain or built up areas had to substitute for genuine strength, but the winkling out of German soldiers could be a very expensive and time consuming business, as one war correspondent reported from the Rhineland: 'Street fighting... is a bad misnomer, because the last place you see any sane man is in a street where every yard is usually covered by a machine gun... The old hands at the game go through a town keeping inside the houses and using bazookas to knock holes in the dividing walls as they go, and when they come to the end of the block and have to cross the street to the next block they throw out smoke and cross under the cover of that. They say it's usually better to clear out a house from the top downwards if you can... Many a man has been hit through freezing and bunching when the trouble starts. You feel inclined to drop down and bury your head, and the next shot gets you; you want to cluster together for mutual company, and in this way you give them a real target.' At Ibbenburen, a group of German officer cadets armed only with rifles accounted for 69 officers and men of 6th Battalion the Highland Light Infantry. Too much of this and Allied troops were inclined to use artillery and grenades, only seeking prisoners later.

By the latter part of the war the quality and strength of German formations was so diverse that a record was being kept of the combat efficiency of divisions which graded them from one to four. The first class were thought fully capable of offensive missions, the fourth class capable of only limited defensive missions. When trained troops ran out, the Volksturm would be called into action. Created in September 1944 as a result of Hitler's decree for 'Total War', this people's militia could in theory call on up to six million male civilians organised in

10,180 battalions in four levies. In practice, only a portion of these saw active service, and though some undoubtedly fought bravely especially in the East, there was a limit to what could be expected of teenagers and old men without transport and adequate weapons. Perhaps their most celebrated stand was made attempting to stem the Soviet tide in Pomerania in February 1945, as was reported by Colonel General Raus: 'With some Panzer support, the backing of anti-tank defences and the support of some artillery, I was confident that 5th *Jäger* [Division] would hold its ground... before assuming command I had issued orders for the construction of a strong system of tank obstacles in the Army's heavily wooded rear area. Those obstacles were defended by *Volksturm* detachments backed up by Army units armed with anti-tank weapons and mounted on bicycles or motorcycles, thus forming groups for immediate offensive action or used defensively to form strong points. The civilian telephone network was taken over and used to give warning of enemy tank movements... These precautions, however satisfactory, represented only a fraction of the total measures which would have been required to resist large scale enemy attacks.' In the resultant battle the defenders would claim the destruction of 580 Soviet tanks, two thirds of them by means of hand-held weapons. The Russians were briefly halted on the Oder – Neisse line, but the war had just two months to run.

THE LEGACY

The Stormtrooper was a creature of his times in that he was born of certain battlefield conditions, and evolved to survive and prosper in a specific hostile environment. The qualities of strength and struggle which he was understood to embody not only spilled over into the civil arena, but came to influence the whole politics of a period. The idea prospered to such an extent that the German army would actually distance itself from some of the

rhetoric, and the Stormtrooper would become an object of vilification for the enemy – as if he was a specific type in his own right.

With May 1945, the 'Stormtrooper' was officially finished, but the basic military ideas which spawned him are still alive wherever there is conflict in the modern world, and are still studied in military staff colleges. Wars still occur, still feature infantry with small arms who hold the ground, still bog down into attrition around trenches and fixed positions. Fire and movement; flexible section tactics; assault rifles; all arms co-operation; assault teams; assault engineers, and soldiers who use their own initiative, all these still have currency in a new millennium.

A moment of success. SS Grenadiers of *Kampfgruppe Hansen* pause to smoke captured American cigarettes near Poteau, Ardennes, December 1944. Note the cold weather clothing, the MG 42, and the close combat knife worn on the chest of the machine gunner.

ARMING THE STORMTROOPER

It has to be said that the basic uniform of the Stormtrooper at the outbreak of World War Two was smart but old fashioned. The 1935 type army *Feldbluse* current for the invasion of Poland was of a greener *Feldgrau* than the essentially monochromatic shade in use in the Great War. It was also distinguished by a bluish green collar and shoulder straps; had four patch pockets with flaps and pleats; belt hooks; and closed to the neck with five pebble textured buttons down the front, though the top button was often left unfastened in the field. The cloth was mainly wool with a small admixture of rayon.

The basic insignia were the breast eagle or *Hoheitsabzeichen* (literally sovereignty badge), the collar *Litzen*, and distinctive shoulder straps. On the issue *Feldbluse* the shoulder straps, or *Schulterklappen*, were separate pieces attached around a small bar of cloth on the shoulder near the top of the sleeve seam, and were fastened by a button near the collar. The straps could convey a number of types of information including the wearer's rank; the arm of service, as for example infantry or artillery; letters or numerals indicating unit or attachment to a staff or instructional school; and occasionally decorative 'tradition badges' and symbols for certain trades or professions. The SS active service units wore either the special model 1937 *Feldbluse* with a field grey collar piped with black and aluminium twisted cord, or the army jacket with addition of the appropriate insignia.

Cold weather saw the use of the great coat, a calf length, traditional, double breasted garment with shoulder straps and a dark blue-green collar. This last was later deleted, being replaced by a particularly deep field grey collar which could be turned up to the nose in bad weather. The service trousers worn at the outbreak of war were usually of a *Steingrau* or stone grey woollen cloth, though from 1940 field grey trousers became more common, and the field jacket was sometimes also worn with the very light grey or off white drill

overalls. Mountain troops were distinguished by the use of climbing trousers and boots, the *Bergmütze* or mountain cap, and the *Edelweiss* arm badge on right upper sleeve.

It was also in 1940 that the uniform began the steady process of simplification under the economies and shortages of war. The *Modell 1940 Feldbluse* was similar to its predecessor except that the collar, and often the shoulder straps, were cut from the ordinary field grey material. From 1942, makers' names were usually deleted from both uniform and personal equipment and replaced with RB code numbers. In 1943, several further simplifications to uniform were officially recognised with the introduction of the *Feldbluse M43*. This garment lacked the pocket pleats, had six buttons instead of five, and was cut from recycled wool commonly mixed with a high percentage of rayon. The collar was usually worn in the open position, and the breast eagle was in a subdued grey rather than white. The new jacket had trousers to match of a practical design which allowed for the use of a belt.

There were a number of subtle variations, in both cut and materials, doubtless because German uniform was now being made in many occupied countries. Impractical side caps were gradually abandoned and instead a peaked ski style M43 cap, similar to that of the mountain troops was made a general issue. Another departure at this time was the issue of the *Schilfgrüner Drillich Felddienstanzug* or reed green drill field service dress. This replaced the old drill issues with a lightweight outfit which doubled as a summer or warm weather combat uniform.

The old style pre-war officer's service dress featured eight buttons; two pleated patch pockets on the breast; two slanted slash pockets at the hips; and deep cuff turnbacks. Though this old style jacket lasted until 1942 and was often retained as a mark of long service, it had been officially replaced, even prior to the outbreak of war, by a

service dress with four pleated pockets and five or six buttons. Officer's uniform could feature not only riding breeches, riding boots, proper linings, distinctive shoulder boards and bullion insignia but was usually individually made up to order. It was therefore better tailored and frequently included minor variations. It was also the case that though peaked caps could be worn by all ranks as a part of walking out dress it was generally only officers and senior NCOs that wore the *Schirmmütze* on service. The varieties were considerable, yet they tended to conform to three major shapes: the old style flat 'plate', 'saddle' form, and the popular soft type which lacked stiffening.

It was only during 1943 that the possibility of completely abandoning the traditional smart jacket was seriously considered, by which time the purity of the cloths used for issue uniform had deteriorated considerably. Economy as well as practicality and modernity now argued for the introduction of a shorter standard uniform jacket. Experiment during the latter part of 1943 led to the evolution of a wool mixture short waisted jacket worn with belted trousers. However, production and issue of the new costume took some time to organise. The *Modell 1944 Felduniform* was not therefore formally introduced until September of that year, but in its own way marked a remarkable departure. Its influences were immediately apparent, for whilst the insignia were essentially economy versions of those already in use, the shape of the garment was highly reminiscent of British 'Battle Dress', and was to a lesser extent similar to some of the clothing of the crews of armoured fighting vehicles.

The basic pattern of the *Model 1944 Feldbluse* was a waist length jacket with a deep waist band with provision for belt hooks, and two large flapped patch pockets on the breast. It was closed with six pebble textured grey painted metal buttons down the front. Interestingly, although the normal colour should have been *Feldgrau 44*, described in

English variously as 'grey brown' or even 'olive brown', the 1944 type uniform appeared in a variety of shades. These included a greenish field grey, and a steely slate grey. This diversity appears to have been caused by the fact that old type cloths of varying qualities remained to be used up, and that a number of fabrics of foreign origin were also utilised. These foreign cloths included a dull grey material from stocks in Italy, and a cloth known as *Russischer–Stoff*. Despite being literally translated as 'Russian material' it is believed that *Russischer–Stoff* was actually a recycled product which used pulped captured Russian uniform as one of its constituents.

BOOTS AND HELMETS

Jack boots or *Marschsteifel* had been well nigh universal for all but specialist troops in 1939, yet ankle boots and gaiters (*Gamaschen*) became progressively more common after the outbreak of war, and there were efforts made to save leather by making the *Marschsteifel* shorter in the leg. From 1943, a new pattern of ankle boot was issued as a matter of course, though both types of footwear continued in use. Both the long and short boots were worn black for much of the war but later on blacking was sometimes omitted with the result that boots were seen in their natural brown colour. The Waffen SS certainly issued orders confirming this practice in 1944.

The Great War steel helmet saw limited use after 1939, but was largely replaced by a new and slightly less bulky model from the mid 1930s. This M 1935 *Stahlhelm* was seen as an improvement in terms of vision and hearing, and lacked the prominent side lugs which had been a feature of earlier models. It was stamped out of a solid piece of metal, between 1.1 and 1.2 mm thick, and featured a crimped rim which created a smooth bottom edge. The liner was of perforated leather held to the helmet shell by means of three rivets. The army helmet initially featured shield shaped

Opposite top, the M35 steel helmet showing the army eagle and swastika insignia.

Opposite bottom, the M36 manoeuvre band in position on the helmet. Four centimetres wide it reversed red and yellow.

Right top, shoulder strap detail on an M44 Feldbluse showing how the detachable strap buttons around a bar of material on the shoulder. The strap is lined with rayon and edged with the *Panzergrenadier* grass green *Waffenfarbe*. *SB*

Right middle, M44 *Feldbluse* detail showing the simplified woven collar *Litzen*, and breast eagle on triangular patch, typical of late war insignia production. *SB*

Above bottom, detail of the M44 jacket interior showing the partial grey lining and the stampings. These include the *Reichsbetriebs Nummer* or 'Reichs business number', and the sizing. Five measurements are given, the top row of figures being waist, chest and collar, the lower the back and sleeve lengths. This is remarkably precise given that British garments of the period were given just approximate chest and height, and an overall size number. *SB*

RANK BADGES IN THE ARMY

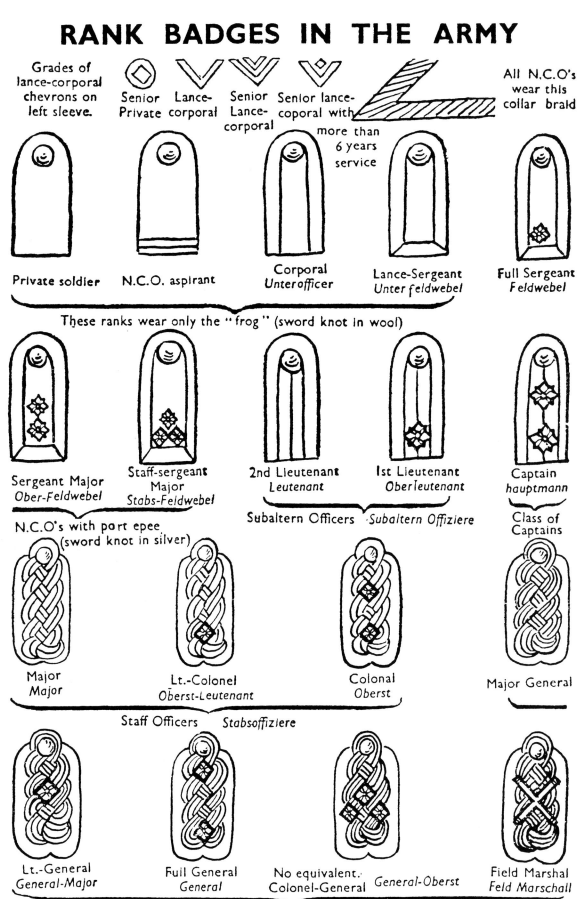

Grades of lance-corporal chevrons on left sleeve.

Senior Private

Lance-corporal

Senior Lance-corporal

Senior lance-corporal with more than 6 years service

All N.C.O's wear this collar braid

Private soldier

N.C.O. aspirant

Corporal *Unterofficer*

Lance-Sergeant *Unterfeldwebel*

Full Sergeant *Feldwebel*

These ranks wear only the "frog" (sword knot in wool)

Sergeant Major *Ober-Feldwebel*

Staff-sergeant Major *Stabs-Feldwebel*

2nd Lieutenant *Leutenant*

1st Lieutenant *Oberleutenant*

Captain *hauptmann*

N.C.O's with port epee (sword knot in silver)

Subaltern Officers *Subaltern Offiziere*

Class of Captains

Major *Major*

Lt.-Colonel *Oberst-Leutenant*

Colonel *Oberst*

Major General

Staff Officers *Stabsoffiziere*

Lt.-General *General-Major*

Full General *General*

No equivalent. Colonel-General *General-Oberst*

Field Marshal *Feld Marschall*

Generals (shoulder pieces in gold and silver)

insignia, with the silver eagle and swastika on the wearers left, and the black, white, red *Reichs* colours on the right. Naval helmets had a gold eagle, the Luftwaffe a flying eagle. The SS *Verfügungstruppe* wore black runes on silver on the right side and a swastika shield in black, white, and red on the other. Myriad other variations existed for organisations such as the police, fire services, and air raid defence. From 1940, the insignia and the helmet itself began to be affected by both economies and the requirements of concealment with the result that from this time the left hand badge was omitted, and minor corners were cut in the production of the helmet. Later this was taken further so that all insignia were deleted, and a 1942 model helmet was produced which lacked the edge crimping. This was easier to produce but left the rim sharp.

Early in the war a rough textured slate grey camouflage paint was issued for use with steel helmets, but there were often local improvisations such as the use of whitewash in winter, or sacking, or even mud in summer. Similarly a wide meshed net was issued for use with foliage or straw, and this had its unofficial equivalents in wire netting, bands of rubber cut from inner tubes and the like, which could be used to hold camouflage. A variety of cloth covers would also see widespread use, the army models usually being made from similar material to the *Zeltbahn*, whilst the SS used a number of distinctive patterns. Perhaps the most famous of these incorporated a long camouflage veil for the use of snipers.

CAMOUFLAGE AND COLD WEATHER CLOTHING

The most interesting aspect of the development of German uniforms during World War Two was the

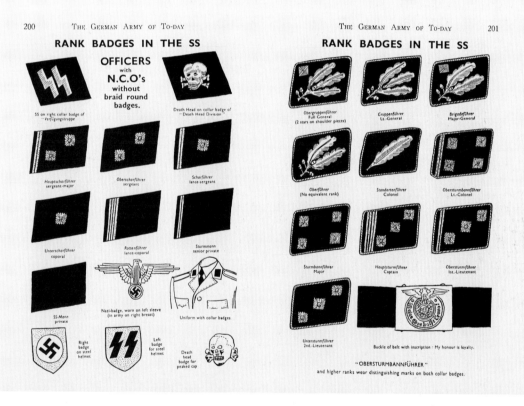

Left, the rank badges of the German army. Note that the 'Waffenfarbe' or arm of service colour of the infantry was white, and that this colour appeared as an edging to the shoulder straps of the other ranks, also being used as a backing colour to the officers' shoulder boards.

Above, the rank badges and other insignia as worn by the Waffen SS as depicted in a British wartime publication.

Right, the wound insignia, or *Verwundeten-Abzeichen*, consisted of an oval badge depicting a steel helmet and crossed swords within a wreath. First introduced in 1918, it was revived during the Spanish Civil War, and again in 1939. In black it signified one or two wounds; in silver three or four; and gold five. Loss of an eye or hand and deafness also qualified for the silver; whilst total disability, blindness, or 'loss of manhood' merited the gold. The general assault badge which appeared in

1940 was originally intended for engineers, but was quickly extended to any assault troops not covered by the infantry assault badge. Special versions were introduced later in the war bearing the numbers '25', '50', '75' or '100' for any veterans who qualified for these numbers of actions. Eight months on the Russian front counted automatically as 10 actions, a year as 15 actions, and 15 months as 25 actions.
From Dich Ruft die SS; Berlin 1942

introduction of many new camouflage and special purpose garments. Though space precludes a detailed description of all, there were many significant innovations. One of the first was the *Windbluse*, the 'wind proof' jacket which had its ancestry amongst the clothing worn by World War One mountain troops. In its basic *Gebirgsjäger* form this was a sage green, double breasted, thigh length coat with four outer pockets with sleeves which could be tightened at the cuffs by means of buttoned tabs. Later a version was introduced which pulled on over the head, was made of field grey cloth, and was provided with a hood, drawstrings, and a row of three large pockets

across the chest, as well as a tail piece which buttoned up under the wearer's crotch.

Camouflage smocks similarly made an early appearance with both theWaffen SS and the army, though their use was by no means uniform. The SS had been the first in the world to use these smocks, the design of which has been credited to *Sturmbannführer* Wim Brant in 1937. They were ultimately worn in a bewildering variety of subtle variations, some of which were the result of intention, others the result of the natural nuances of the screen printing and machine printing processes which were used. The basic Waffen SS design, however, was reversible and featured a loose

Above, recreated infantry-man of 1944 wearing the *Zeltbahn* and helmet with net waits under cover of a bank. Note how the net may be pulled down to obscure the face; the wearing of the leather equipment over the poncho; and the metal containers for smoke grenades and machine gun ammunition.
M. Seed

Right, recreated infantry Grenadier of 1943, showing the *Zeltbahn* worn as a poncho, with the Model 1935 steel helmet and Kar 98k rifle. *SB*

Far right, reconstruction showing the wearing of the Model 1930 gas mask and steel helmet with camouflage net. *MS*

Recreation showing a 1944 dated snow camouflage coat worn over the 1943 field uniform by a *Volksgrenadier*. The coat is a well made factory produced garment with size markings. The Kar 98k carbine is of typical wartime manufacture. *SB*

Recreated *Volksgrenadier* of 1944 showing the Schnee *Tarnungüberzug* or snow camouflage coat worn with the hood over the steel helmet. The uniform jacket is the *Feldbluse 43* with simplified grey *Litzen* at the collar. *SB*

collarless shape, laced neck closure, and gathered waist and cuffs. The early garments which had been intended for wear over the equipment had a low waist and vertical openings on either side of the body through which ammunition and the like could be accessed. Later on it was recognised that smocks were more conveniently worn under the belt, with the result that they were made with a higher waist and a pair of external pockets. SS smocks were generally of spotty or blotchy patterns, greener on one side, browner on the other, to change with the season. The major configurations have since been dubbed 'plane tree', 'palm tree', and 'oak leaf' patterns. Army garments

were usually distinguishable by the use of the *Splittermuster*, or 'splinter' camouflage pattern, reversible to white, which was later supplemented by the *Sumpfmuster*, or marsh pattern.

Cold weather clothing, generally limited to great coats, pullovers, woollen gloves, toques, animal skins, and blanket-lined watch coats prior to 1941, became a critical requirement after the Soviet invasion. The first modern, padded, reversible winter combat uniform was demonstrated to Hitler in 1942, and was in production soon after. It consisted of a thigh length hooded jacket and trousers with braces. The shell of the garment was cotton and rayon, whilst the padding was of cellulose wool.

Prisoners after the Allied Rhine crossing, Germany, March 1945. A mixture of uniforms are worn, but two good examples of the M 44 ensemble appear in the front rank. The 1944 type *Feldbluse* is worn open necked with scarf or roll top sweater, one man having an Iron Cross ribbon through a button hole. Note also the belted trousers, gaiters worn with ankle boots, and the M 43 *Einheitsfeldmütze*.

Initially it was grey on one side, white on the other, but soon the grey was changed to either 'splinter' or 'marsh' pattern camouflage. Though the ordinary winter suit was worn by the SS, it was predictable that they would introduce their own version shortly afterwards. This had a spotted brown or green camouflage on one side, and was white on the other.

The winter uniform could be layered with the basic uniform, sweaters, padded waistcoats, fur under jackets, and long underwear. Over mittens, with or without 'trigger fingers', and felt boots completed the ensemble. The felt boots were of two main varieties. A huge and rather surgical looking type which dated back to the Great War and incorporated a thick wooden sole and closed with two buttoned straps was intended to be worn over the ordinary footwear, normally by sentries. A slightly more elegant looking version was marginally smaller and thinner, worn with socks only, and more amenable to marching.

It has generally been assumed that most snow camouflage garments were improvisations, with an emphasis on bed sheets and ingenuity. Though this was sometimes the case, particularly in the early part of the war, there were many patterns of factory produced clothes available in different size fittings for the purpose. One of the most impressive garments was the Schnee *Tarnung Überzug*,

a long buttoned coat with attached hood which was provided with small pleats to improve fit, and slash openings through which the equipment could be accessed underneath. It was well made yet impractical for crawling or vigorous movement. Perhaps for these reasons it was supplemented by the *Schneeanzüge*, a two-piece suit with jacket and trousers; snow shirts and smocks which were shorter than the long coat and pulled on over the head, and one-piece overalls. These last were not unlike a loose white boiler suit gathered at the ankles. There was also a light, white version of the *Windbluse* complete with three buttoned pockets across the chest, hood, draw strings and crotch piece.

Snow camouflage helmet covers were likewise both factory and locally produced, and the improvised varieties included both rough squares of fabric held in place by a band and types which were gathered under the brim. The factory produced examples were properly fabricated and incorporated a drawstring to ensure a good fit. Splinter pattern covers were also made reversible to white. In one version of the single-sided white cover, a fine gauze face veil was incorporated, and though this helped obscure the telltale dark blob of the face, it was difficult to see distant objects through it.

A veteran wearing the six buttoned Model 1943 *Feldbluse* utility cap and wound badge on the left breast. *SB*

Portrait of a typical German soldier circa 1944. The *Einheitsfeldmütze*, or utility cap, was introduced in June 1943. The jacket is the *Modell 1943 Feldbluse*, a garment of relatively poor quality. *SB*

A war time studio portrait, circa 1942, of an infantryman wearing the *Modell 1934* field cap. This headgear was often known as the *Schiffschen*, or 'little ship'. It bears the eagle, a chevron of white *Waffenfarbe*, and cockade. The 1935 *Feldbluse* has been customised by pressing open the collar. *SB*

PERSONAL EQUIPMENT

The usual other ranks personal equipment or *Feldausrüstung* of 1939 was based around a black leather belt, the buckle of which bore an eagle and swastika and the wording *Gott Mit Uns*. Riflemen wore a bayonet in leather frog, and model 1911 cartridge pouches. These pouches or *Patronentasche Modell 1911*, which had originally been introduced for cavalry, were adopted generally by the army in 1933 and had three small pockets with individual fastenings, the complete set of two pouches accommodating a total of 60 rounds. Sometimes, particularly in support units, only one pouch was worn. Troops armed with machine pistols wore one or two special belt pouches, each capable of accommodating three stick magazines. These pouches were initially of black leather, but later economy versions in green canvas became commonplace. Similarly many other support straps were similarly substituted by woven or folded canvas. Ammunition carriers for the *Sturmgewehr* or assault rifle, also accommodated three magazines, but were distinguished by their size and distinctive curved shape.

The basic belt kit usually included the bread bag or *Brotbeutel Modell 1931*, and water bottle. Fat or butter was held in a circular Bakelite container which varied from almost black to orange in colour.

Field rations were prepared by mobile kitchens, and individual tinned 'iron rations' were bulked with bread, biscuit and sausage where available, yet problems with food supply would ultimately prove as difficult as at the end of the Great War. By the middle of the Second World War, *Wehrmacht Suppe*, the main ingredients of which were water and potatoes, was being served on every conceivable occasion.

Two main types of entrenching tool were carried, the old pattern with its short rigid handle, and the *Klappspaten*, or folding spade, which was made a more effective implement by its longer handle and more pointed blade, being introduced in 1938. The folding spade could also be used like a mattock when its head was locked at right angles. The carriers for these tools, which were suspended by two loops from the belt, were of black leather, or later black or brown *Press-Stoff* leather substitute. When the cylindrical gas mask canister or *Tragbüchse für Gasmaske* was worn by infantry this was usually suspended by a long strap around the neck and shoulder, a short tag with suspender helped steady the bottom end of the canister on the belt. The *Gasplane* or gas sheet, which was intended as a protection against blister gases, was carried in a dark bluish green wallet, and was worn either on the gas mask case strap or secured to the

A pair of 1911 Model ammunition pouches, shown back and front. MS

A typical selection of field mess equipment shown on a smoke grenade box. Top left, the mess tin or Kochgeschirr 31; top right, the water bottle Feldflasche 31, and drinking cup; bottom right, folding cutlery. Centre right is the folding solid fuel Esbit stove. This was carried folded with small fuel blocks inside, but when needed it was unfolded and a container placed on top, the blocks were then lit, heating the food or drink. The cylindrical yellowish brown bakelite container, front centre, is the *Fettbüchse* or 'fat box' for lard or butter. These items and others would be carried in, or alongside, the issue bread bag. *MS*

Above, detail of the Kar 98k rifle, shown with the rifle cleaning kit, pull through, brush, oiler and field dressing. The *Tornister* and bag from the assault pack occupy the background. *MS*

Opposite, reconstruction showing typical field equipment, c 1943. The belt carries the entrenching tool, bayonet, water bottle and bread bag. The assault pack is attached to the support straps (*Koppeltraggestell*) and holds the mess tin and *Zeltbahn. SB*

mask canister.

Full marching order required the use of a back pack. The 1934 type *Tornister* was a green or tan canvas pack with shoulder straps and a flap adorned with natural cow hide retaining its hair surface. The shelter sheet and great coat could be carried strapped around the pack. From 1938, a new model *Tornister* began to appear which was similar, but did not have integral shoulder straps, and therefore required the use of distinctive 'Y' shaped suspenders or belt supports, known as *Koppeltraggestell*, which came up over the shoulders and attached to the tops of the ammunition pouches at the front.

In April 1939, a special combat pack was introduced which was more suited to the vigorous exertion of the assault; and similarly required the use of separate support straps. This *Gefechtsgepäck* was a simple light 'A' shaped frame to which various pieces of equipment could be attached. Very often this included a small rectangular canvas bag containing items like the rifle cleaning kit and rations; also the shelter sheet; and the mess tin or *Kochgeshirr*. Specialist packs were also worn by other assault troops. Mountain troops wore a Bergen style canvas rucksack with leather straps, and rucksacks were also more generally issued, especially on the Eastern Front after the invasion of Russia. The *Pioneersturmgepäck* or pioneer assault pack, was introduced in 1941 and consisted of an oblong canvas bag worn on the separate support straps, usually combined with side pouches worn on the belt. This equipment was designed to accommodate explosives, grenades, and the gas mask.

The *Modell 1931 Zeltbahn* or tent sheet was one of the most versatile and useful pieces of the soldier's equipment. It consisted of a large triangular piece of camouflage printed waterproof gabardine cloth with a slit in the middle and metal buttons around the edge. It could be slipped over the head and worn loose as a simple poncho; buttoned around the legs for marching cycling or riding; used as a groundsheet; used as part of the bed roll; or used as a part of a tent. Two sheets made a simple bivouac, four sheets a pyramid-shaped four man tent.

As might be expected, massive expansion of the forces and shortages of materials considerably stretched the supply of all types of equipment. The use of substitute materials has been touched on, but lack of equipment also tended to blur the distinctions between the special patterns supposedly issued to special formations like the Luftwaffe and Waffen SS, and brought into use many pieces which were manufactured in occupied countries, or were captured from the enemy. Particularly common in the field were items such as Austrian and Polish made entrenching tools, Soviet tent sections, and pouches made to match captured weapons.

RIFLES

The main arm in 1939 was the bolt action Kar 98 k carbine. Though production had started as recently as 1934 the basic design was anything but new since most of the fundamentals, including the five round magazine, were shared with the G98 which had seen service in the Great War. The biggest difference was undoubtedly the 60 cm barrel, a length which had been suggested by experience in the trenches and confirmed by *Reichsheer* experiment as the best compromise for maximum handiness with minimum muzzle blast whilst retaining reasonable range and accuracy.

The common Mauser type bayonet fitting, leather sling and cleaning rod were retained. The usual bayonet was the *Seitengewehr 84/98* which had been introduced for use with carbines during the Great War, and had in fact equipped many of the *Sturmbatallione*. It was relatively short, with a blade 25 cm long, was therefore handy, and could at a pinch be used as a combat knife, though purpose

Opposite,
Inserting the detonator into the *Steilhandgranate 39*. The Second World War stick grenade was essentially similar to its First World War ancestor, but lacked the belt hook and had a four and a half second delay; the basic grenade could also be fitted with a fragmentation sleeve. The *Nebelhandgranat 39* was like the high explosive bomb in appearance, but generated smoke. Note the camouflage smock and helmet cover. *IWM MH 9234*

made *Nahkampfmesser* were also widely produced. Originally the Kar 98k rifle was stocked in solid walnut or beech, but during the war many were made with stocks of a laminated construction. This both saved on good wood and proved more resistant to warping. The Kar 98 k was produced in huge numbers but even so necessity dictated the continued use of a number of other rifles including the old G98, the Kar 98b, and the G33 / 40 which was an adaption of a Czechoslovak carbine

Though good so far as it went, the Kar 98k was old even as it appeared, and as war began, a scramble commenced to find a semi-automatic with which it could be replaced. The immediate result was the *Gewehr 41*, a semi-automatic rifle with a ten-shot magazine. This worked well enough, yet was heavy, not very well balanced and difficult to make. Thus it was that although the G41 saw use on the Eastern Front, it was never a practical replacement. An improved G43 model fared rather better, was produced in larger numbers, and was fitted to take a telescope so it could also be used for sniping, but it was clear that the basic concept had its limitations, particularly as an assault weapon.

The answer appeared to be something which combined the handiness and firepower of a sub-machine gun with the accuracy of a rifle. This was not as easy to achieve as might appear at first glance, the main stumbling block being that normal rifle ammunition becomes just too much to handle when going off on full automatic in the hands of a charging infantryman. The best success that was achieved using the ordinary cartridge was the FG 42 designed for parachutists, though this was still essentially an ultra lightweight, light machine gun, with the benefit of a box magazine. On the other hand, pistol ammunition, as used in most sub-machine guns, was not really of much more than localised effect.

A new class of gun therefore required a new type of ammunition: as was realised by Vollmer and others even before the war, but it was only with the development of the 7.9 mm *Infanterie Kurz Patrone* or infantry short cartridge, that a round was found which was reliable for full automatic use, accurate to a decent range, and could reasonably be fired on the move. With this, a quantum leap was achieved. The first weapon to use the new round was the *Maschinenpistole 42*, yet despite the name, the MP 42 was no sub-machine gun, but very nearly, in one fell swoop, the development of the modern assault rifle. The name was said to have been camouflage, to hide it from the Allies, and to disguise its development from Hitler, who had an aversion both to the introduction of a new cartridge at a critical time, and to infantry weapons which had less than the maximum possible range.

Various modifications and *Ostfront* trials later, the MP 42 evolved into the MP 43 and finally into the *Sturmgewehr 44* – meaning literally 'assault rifle 1944'. Practically and psychologically, the new assault rifle certainly lived up to its name, and the troops that carried it were taught to fire semi-automatically under normal circumstances, turning to bursts of full automatic when the situation required. The result was both increased firepower and considerable versatility since the new weapon could do most things that a rifle or a sub-machine could do, and more besides. The weapon had decent power and accuracy to 600 metres, a 30-round detachable box magazine, and a practical rather than elegant finish. Total production was thought to be a little under half a million.

MACHINE WEAPONS

Central to all infantry squad tactics was the light machine gun. Though relatively small numbers of old weapons remained in service, the mainstay of the German army in World War Two was the *Maschinengewehr 34*. What made this gun special was that when it was introduced in 1936, it was one of the first truly 'general purpose' machine guns. Mounted on the *Maschinengewehr-Lafette 34*

Opposite, cleaning the *Karabiner 98k*. Despite technological advances and the introduction of automatic 'assault rifles', the majority of the infantry were still using bolt action Mausers at the end of World War Two. Total production of the Kar 98k was believed to be well in excess of 10,000,000. *SB*

Mountain troops using
the MG 42. Also visible
are the *Edelweiss* badge;
metal ammunition belt
box, and the *Windjacke
für Gebirgstruppen*, or
'wind proof jacket for
mountain troops'.

tripod it was capable of steady and sustained support fire to ranges over 3000 metres. For squad work it was fitted with a bipod, and could use either belts or drums. It was also widely used as an anti-aircraft weapon, and on vehicle mountings. According to Helmut Pabst its relatively high cyclic rate made it easily distinguishable from the Russian Maxims: 'The Russian machine guns have a dull coughing sound, while ours make a high whipping noise.' In the 'light' infantry role, the MG 34 weighed only a little over 12 kg, and remained accurate to 800 metres.

The MG 34 was good, but time consuming to produce, so in May 1942 a new weapon was introduced which was arguably even better. The MG 42 was light and made use of cheaper stampings, yet its most apparent feature was its amazing 1200 rounds per minute cyclic rate. Though better used in short bursts, *in extremis* it could burn its way through a 250 round belt in under 15 seconds with a sound like tearing fabric. The main advantage of this phenomenal rate of fire was its effectiveness against fleeting targets, and the wall of lead which could be thrown up against aircraft.

The demand for machine guns as a primary weapon of both defence and attack was well nigh insatiable, with each infantry division establishment requiring 643 machine guns, a figure which was upped to 656 in 1944. Motorised divisions could dispose of as many as 1,101 machine guns. The result was that many obsolete weapons such as the MG 08, MG 08 / 15, MG 13 and MG 15 were all seen in limited use, particularly in defensive formations. Foreign guns were also to be seen from time to time, as for example the Austrian Schwarzlose which was rechristened the MG 7 / 12 (ö), and the Czech VZ 37 'Besa' which became the MG 37 (cz). Both of these were adequate tripod mounted stop gaps. The Czech ZB light machine gun, which went primarily to the Waffen SS was in a superior category, having already served as the primary inspiration for the Bren gun. Other oddities which saw service included the old Danish designed Madsen, and the Swedish designed and not terribly reliable Knorr-Bremse which equipped some of the foreign units of the Waffen SS.

In terms of sub-machine guns, the Germans were in advance of much of the world in 1939. Several different Bergmann types had been produced by this time, and the MP 35 for example now went primarily to the SS. Yet the newest, and arguably the best weapon was the MP 38, now being produced for the army. Though commonly dubbed the *Schmeisser*, Hugo Schmeisser actually had little to do with its design, which was produced by Erma as a result of the Spanish Civil War. It featured a 32 round box magazine, reasonable performance, innovative resin grips and folding skeleton stock: indeed, considering the relative lack of competition it was excellent. The biggest problem was producing enough of these weapons, and to avoid leaving many squad leaders permanently equipped with Bergmanns or rifles, the design of the MP 38 was modified for simplicity. The result was the MP 40. Even so, new tactics involving whole units armed with sub-machine guns and the use of such weapons by occupation forces meant that demand continued to rise. This was partly offset by the use of sub-machine guns produced in other Axis states, such as the Italian Beretta, partly met by continuing to use obsolete models such as the MP 28, and partly by reusing many of the captured Russian weapons.

PISTOLS AND GRENADES

Though the P08 'Luger' pistol continued in use throughout the Second World War, a new weapon had been adopted for the army in 1938 in the shape of the 9mm Walter P38. This was intended to be more robust, and easier to produce, and also offered the advantage of a double action trigger. This meant that the gun could be loaded and cocked, and then put on safety with the hammer

Next page, despite new weapons many units had to make do with the last generation of technology. This official *Wehrmacht Bildserie* illustration shows the MG 08 with ZF 12 optical sight still in limited use in the Second World War. *SB*

1) The *Maschinenpistole 43*. This remarkable weapon was one of the first true 'assault' rifles, with a 30 round magazine, capable of full automatic fire during the attack, and aimed fire to about 600 metres. Key to the system was a short 7.92 mm round, making the weapon more easy to handle than a light machine gun, yet more accurate than a sub-machine gun. In 1944 a slightly modified model was christened the *Sturmgewehr* – literally assault rifle. The similarity with many modern assault rifles is unmistakable.
TRH Pictures –
MOD Pattern Room

2) The *Leuchtpistole*, literally 'light pistol', was the standard flare gun in use with German forces during World War Two. Made of a light alloy it broke open rather like a shot gun to accept a single 26 mm signal cartridge. Aimed skywards and discharged it would launch one of a number of coloured signals composed of coloured stars or smoke puffs. Small grenades were also produced for this weapon.

3 & 4) *Pistole, Modell 35 (p)* and holster. First produced in 1936 for Polish forces, and originally known as the Radom or Vis, this 9mm semi-automatic was a reliable weapon based on the Browning system. After the fall of Poland, manufacture was continued by the Germans to help meet the huge demand for weapons, being particularly favoured by the SS and parachute troops. The Radom was just one of many weapons produced in occupied countries and used by German forces.

Opposite, recreation of a Panzergrenadier, 1944. Note the MP 40 submachine gun; helmet with camouflage net; *Feldbluse M44*; ankle boots and drill trousers both of the 1943 type. The gloves are of the grey wool issue variety size being denoted by white rings inside the cuff. *SB*

lowered, but that the next pull on the trigger both raised and released the hammer without further preparation. The P38 featured an eight round magazine, proved accurate and easy to shoot, and perhaps most importantly continued to function in the cold of the Eastern Front.

Despite the success of the P38 and continued production of the P08, handguns remained in pitifully short supply. The result was that German forces used myriad Behelfspistol, or substitutes, from a bewildering variety of sources for combat formations as well as the rear echelons. One venerable pistol to see re-use was the old Mauser C96 'Broomhandle'. This appeared not only in its usual semi automatic form but in a Schnellfeuer full automatic model which saw limited use with the *Waffen* SS. This doubtless had a certain surprise value but was no match for a genuine sub-machine gun. Other German weapons which saw service included the Walther PP; PPK; Sauer; and Mauser HSc semi automatics, all in 7.65 mm.

Foreign pistols also saw widespread use. Perhaps the best of these were the Browning Model 1935, and the Polish Radom. The Browning was being manufactured in Belgium at the time of the German invasion, and this excellent gun continued to be produced as the *Pistole Modell 35 (b)*. Many went to SS and parachute formations,

where its reliability, 9mm parabellum cartridge and 13-round magazine capacity were much appreciated. The Polish *Radom*, which entered German service as the *Pistole Modell 35 (p)* was likewise based on a Browning design, was similarly chambered for 9mm, and was a remarkably robust gun with an eight-round capacity. Also seen in some numbers was the 9mm Austrian *Steyr Model 1912*, which in a very slightly modified form became the *Pistole Modell 12 (ö)*. This was a useful weapon whose only significant drawback was an integral eight-shot magazine which could prove awkward to load.

Grenades were a staple of close action combat from 1939, and the basic M24 and M39 stick grenades were essentially similar to the Great War predecessor, having a wooden handle through which a pull cord was fitted, a detonator, and a metal cylinder head containing the explosive charge. One small refinement was the optional fitting of a metal sleeve around the grenade

The *Sturmgewehr* in action in the Ardennes, December 1944. The large triple pouch for magazines is worn on the soldier's right side. Notice also the SS camouflage jacket in the spotted or 'pea' pattern.

head for better fragmentation. The *Nebelhandgranat 39* was a variation on the theme, being a stick smoke grenade, ideal for creating screens during the assault. As the war progressed other varieties of stick grenade made their appearance. The *Steilhangranate 43* was a conventional high explosive bomb differing only in the fact that the igniter formed part of the head rather than the handle. The *Behelfshandranate Holz* was again a stick grenade, but something of an emergency measure in that it was completely made of wood and relied on blast for its effect. The *Nipolit* stick bomb was a much more interesting innovation of the last few months of the war. This had no head casing at all, for the head was actually moulded from a form of plastic explosive.

As in the Great War, handy egg-shaped bombs were also widely used. The *Eierhangranate 39* was actually a little larger than its predecessor, and had a body made of thin metal with a small pull knob igniter on the top. It was sometimes fitted with an extra fragmentation cover. The knob was pulled, the bomb thrown, and exploded between four and five seconds later. Such bombs were frequently to be seen hung from the equipment, though theoretically the small rings with which they were provided were for attaching them to each other, or to a target.

MORTARS

Though mortars were often used to harass, they could be every bit as effective as artillery under the right circumstance, as was recorded by *Hauptsturmführer* Schiller of the *SS Liebstandarte*, in Russia: 'I was just trying to move 200 metres ahead in order to look out over the surrounding terrain where my men were, when the first salvo hit. I threw myself into one of the foxholes the Russians had left behind, but I must have had my left leg sticking up in the air, for a mortar shell landing to the right of me tore my left foot off without giving

Back blast and dust created by a *Panzerschreck* anti-tank team, 1944. The *Panzerschreck* fired an 8.8 cm rocket to an effective range of about 150 metres and was capable of dealing with most tanks.
TRH Pictures

me any other wound. Hofrichter was immediately at my side and tied off my calf with a strip of *Zeltbahn* after I had cut off the tatters of my pants leg with a pocket knife. Because of the shock I experienced no pain. So when the stretcher bearers carrying me had to stop because of the heat, I was able to hop a little ways'. The German army used mortars of many different descriptions; and several formed an integral part of assault formations.

The basic light mortar issued to platoons was the *Granatenwerfer 36*, a 5cm model, well engineered, even over engineered, and capable of throwing brisk fusillades of small bombs up to 500 metres in support of attacks. Next up the scale was the *Granatenwerfer 34*. This was deployed with the company heavy weapons platoon, usually in three subsections, each of two mortars. Though the total complement was seven, including the detachment commander and mortar commander, the weapon could quite easily be fired by two men once emplaced and supplied with bombs. It was capable of firing once every four or five seconds for short periods, throwing a 3.5 kg bomb to 2,500 metres. For transit the equipment could be broken down into three loads, each weighing about 18 kg.

ANTI-TANK WEAPONS

Like most nations in 1939, Germany's infantry anti-armour capability was based on anti-tank rifles. The *Panzerbüchse 38* and *39* were both single-shot 13 mm rifles, which had much in common with their Great War ancestor the *T-Gewehr*. Under ideal conditions they were capable of penetrating about 30 mm of armour and would have been tolerably effective had not tanks been making rapid developmental advances at the same time. A monstrously heavy semi-automatic anti-tank rifle was introduced in 1941, but this made no impact whatsoever on the Russian T-34, and was rapidly discarded.

There was now a rapid scramble to create more potent hand held weapons including charges which had to be placed on the enemy vehicle and anti-tank rifle grenades. These were backed by improvisations such as the old 'concentrated charge' made up of seven stick grenade heads, Molotov cocktails; mines thrown in front of tanks; and, perhaps most alarmingly, smoke grenades attached to 20-litre petrol cans. The suicidally brave tied two smoke grenades together with a cord and lobbed the contraption over the gun barrels of the enemy tanks, thereby blinding them and allowing other troops the chance to get close. Hollow charges attached by magnets did prove devastating if they found their target and were probably the best of the bunch, but none of these methods was very satisfactory.

Too often the result of ineffective anti-tank weapons was disaster; just one example of many was provided by Joachim Wieder at Stalingrad: 'A grey-white row of the dreaded T-34 tanks came rolling along the side of our petrified column, but their cannon and machine guns did not fire... A Soviet soldier in a white coat, maybe a Commissar, sat on the leading tank, waving to us and calling in broken German, "German soldier, come, come! Hitler kaputt! " Suddenly the Russian rolled forward over the body of the tank mortally hit by a bullet. From somewhere, someone threw a bottle filled with inflammable liquid that the soldiers called a "Molotov Cocktail" and set the leading tank on fire. Now our fate had been set in motion. The hatches slammed shut, the tanks rattled back apace and then opened a murderous fire... The short bark of the cannon, the tacking of the machine guns and the zipping and whistling of the rounds surrounded us like music from hell while we sought cover in the holes and slits of the roadbed and tremblingly waited to be crushed...'

Sometimes the problem was neither the inadequacy of the weapons, nor lack of determination in their use but over enthusiasm mixed with inexperience, as Helmut Pabst noticed at the beginning of 1943: 'One day our battalion

Opposite, the crew of an 81 mm *Granatenwerfer 34*, Normandy 1944. The man in the foreground left is wearing the M39 frame for carrying heavy equipment; all have heavy camouflage breaking up the outline of their helmets. TRH Pictures

The 81 mm mortar or *Granatenwerfer 34* in action, Belgium 1940. Deployed with the heavy weapons company of the infantry battalion, this mortar was capable of rapid fire to 2500 metres. It could be broken down into three loads and used from positions inaccessible to field guns. TRH Pictures

shot up eighteen tanks before Beshenki. At Martinovo there were twenty knocked out on a front of three hundred yards. In the woods before Tabrakovo they had to decide by rota who was allowed to take on the next, because in the beginning they all ran after them – the major, the adjutant and the duty officer – leaving the command post deserted. Even the sergeant of the anti-tank gun left his weapon and joined in the hunt with a limpet mine. And the tanks came day after day. Day after day the companies got smaller... But our Bavarians fought to the death.' Tank hunting was not just a matter of courage and material, but of skill, training and tactics, as was explained to the soldiery by means of a quirky cartoon publication entitled *Der Panzerknacker*. Slowly the infantry versus armour balance would begin to shift.

The first really effective hand-held anti-tank weapon reached the troops in early 1943. The *Panzerfaust* or 'tank fist' was novel in that it linked a simple tubular projector with a hollow charge projectile which was propelled by black powder. It was crude, one shot only, and at first limited to only 30 metres range, but certainly beat having to charge the enemy tank, and was capable of a respectable 140 mm armour penetration. Subsequent models upped the range to 150 metres and penetration to 200 mm, enough to deal with pretty well any Allied tank. The weapon was hopefully dubbed the 'Grenadier's anti-tank gun' by propagandists. Though prone to damp and still requiring courage, the *Panzerfaust* was a remarkable device, and towards the end of the war production would reach a million a month. Even though only a fraction of these struck enemy tanks they made a considerable contribution in helping to offset the Allied preponderance in armour.

A weapon of greater technical sophistication was the reloadable *Panzerschreck* or *Raketenpanzerbüchse*, development of which was aided by early captures of the American Bazooka. Arguably the *Panzerschreck* went one better, being an 88 mm rocket launcher incorporating electronic ignition. The first model reached the troops in the summer of 1943, and proved capable of penetrating 160 mm of armour at 160 metres, static infantry positions could be engaged at several hundred metres. Like all recoiless rocket weapons it had a vicious back blast but its most significant drawback was the belch of flaming particles which could burn the unwary, and contributed to its nickname *Ofenrohr*, or 'stove pipe'. Until an improved version with a shield appeared, operators were well advised to wear gas mask and helmet.

Opposite, the 1935 model light flamethrower in practice against a block house. Consisting essentially of two reservoirs containing respectively combustible fuel and a propellant, a hose, and a means of ignition, the flamethrower was a Pionier weapon ideal for close range attack. Though limited to a range of about 25 metres and about ten short squirts of fire it was ideal for confined spaces where asphyxiation and terror would multiply its effect. *TRH Pictures*

Next page, a Wehrmacht official photograph showing the MG 34 on its sustained fire mount. This view shows the bipod folded, the use of the optical sight, and a spare barrel. The crew have pre-war uniforms distinguishable by their pointed shoulder straps, and insignia on both sides of the steel helmets. *SB*

Military Illustrated is the leading monthly military history magazine in the English language. Since its inception, it has built up an unrivalled reputation among military historians, enthusiasts, collectors, re-enactors, and military modellers for authoritative articles, primary research, rare photographs, and specially commissioned artwork spanning the entire history of warfare from ancient to modern — including the most popular periods such as World Wars Two and One, Napoleonic Wars, and ancient and medieval combat.

Copies of the magazine are available on newsstands and in specialist shops or can be obtained directly from the publisher on subscription from:

Military Illustrated
45 Willowhayne Avenue
East Preston
West Sussex
BN16 1PL
Great Britain
Tel: 01903 775121

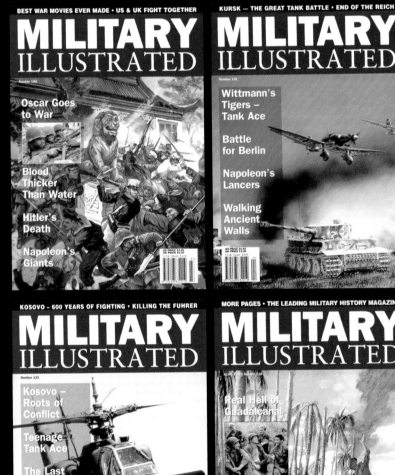

BIBLIOGRAPHY

Ailsby C. *World War II German Medals.*
London, 1994

Angolia J.R. & Schlicht A. *Uniforms and
Traditions of the German Army.* 3 vols.
San Jose, 1984, 1986

Army Officer Recruitment Office *Offizier
Im Grossdeutschen Heer.* Berlin, undated

Armin S.v. *Experiences of the IV. German
Army Corps in the Battle of the Somme.*
English Trans. GHQ 1916

Baer L. *The History of the German
Steel Helmet.* San Jose, 1985

Baird J.W. *To Die For Germany.*
Bloomington,1990

Barker A.J. *Waffen SS at War.*
London, 1982

Barker C.R. & Last R.W. *Erich Maria
Remarque.* London, 1979

Barnett C. *The Swordbearers.*
London, 1963

Barnett C. ed. *Hitler's Generals.*
London, 1989

Bartov O. *Hitler's Army.* Oxford, 1991

Beevor A. *Stalingrad.* London, 1998

Bruce R. *Machine Guns of World War I.*
London, 1997

Buchner A. *Der Minenkrieg Auf Vauquois.*
Karlsfeld, 1982

Buchner A. *Das Handbuch Der Deutschen
Infanterie, 1939-1945.* Friedberg, 1989

Bull S.B. *German Army Uniforms,
World War I.* London, 1999

Carell P. *Scorched Earth.* Boston, 1970

Carr W. *A History of Germany.* London, 1969

Carter A. *German Bayonets; the Models
98/02 and 98/05.* Norwich, 1984

Dane E. *Trench Warfare.* London, 1915

Davis B.L. *Badges and Insignia of the
Third Reich.* Poole, 1983

Davis B.L. *German Army Uniforms
and Insignia.* London, 1971

Ebelshauser G.A. *The Passage.* R.
Baumgartner ed. Huntington, 1984

Einsiedel H. v. *The Onslaught.*
London, 1984

Ellis C. *German Infantry and Assault
Engineer Equipment.* King's Langley, 1976

Ellis J. *The Sharp End.* Newton Abbot, 1980

English J.A. *A Perspective on Infantry.* New
York, 1981

Erickson J. *The Road to Stalingrad.* London,
1993

Erlam D. *Ranks and Uniforms of the
German Army, Navy and Airforce.*
London, c. 1940

D'Este C. *Decision in Normandy.*
London, 1983

'Factus' *Uniforms, Badges and Intelligence
Data of the German Forces.* London, c. 1940

Falkenhayn E. v. *General Headquarters
1914-1916 and its Critical Decisions.*
London, 1919

Farrar-Hockley A. *Infantry Tactics,
1939-1945.* New Malden, 1976

Feldgrau *Feldgrau Journal of German Army
Uniform and Organisation.*

Fisch R. *Field Equipment of the Infantry.*
Sykesville, 1989

Fleischer W. *German Trench Mortars
and Infantry Mortars.* Atglen, 1996

Fleischer W. *Panzerfaust.* Atglen, 1994

Franke, Frise, Graf and Kabisch *Unser
Kampf in Holland, Belgien, und Flandern.*
München, 1941

Franke H. *Handbuch der Neuzeitlichen
Wehrwissenschaften.* Berlin, 1937

Gajkowski M. *German Squad Tactics of
World War II.* West Chester, 1995

General Staff German *Experiences in the
Winter Battle in Champagne.* 1915

General Staff German *Proposals for the
Technical Methods to be Adopted in an
Attempt to Break Through.* 1915

General Staff German *Flammenwerfer.*
1916

General Staff German *Nahkampfmittel:
Weapons of Close Combat.* 1917

General Staff UK *Extracts From German
Documents and Correspondence.* 1916

General Staff UK *German Raid on the
British Trenches Near La Boisselle.* 1916

General Staff UK *German Instructions
Regarding Gas Warfare.* 1916

General Staff UK *Notes on German Army
Corps.* 1916

General Staff UK *Summary of Recent
Information Regarding the German Army.*
1917

General Staff UK *Handbook of the
German Army in War.* 1918

General Staff UK *The German Forces in
the Field.* 1918

General Staff US *Histories of the Two
Hundred and Fifty One Divisions of the
German Army.* 1919

Goldsmith D.L. *The Devil's Paintbrush.*
Toronto, 1989

Goodspeed D.J. *Ludendorff.* London, 1966

Götz H.D. *German Military Rifles and
Machine Pistols 1871-1945.* English Trans,
West Chester, 1990

Griffith P. *Battle Tactics of the Western
Front.* Yale, 1994

Griffith P. *Forward into Battle.*
Chichester, 1981

Guderian H. *Panzer Leader.* English Trans
London, 1952

Gudmundsson B.I. *Stormtroop Tactics:
Innovation in the German Army, 1914-1918.*
New York, 1989

Haber L.F. *The Poisonous Cloud.*
Oxford, 1986

Hamelman W.E. *German Wound Badges.*
Dallas, undated

Hart B.H.L. *The Other Side of the Hill.*
London, 1948

Hartmann T. *Wehrmacht Divisional Signs.*
London, 1970

Herwig H.H. *The First World War: Germany
and Austria Hungary.* London, 1997

Hettler E. *Uniformen Der Deutschen
Wehrmacht.* c. 1940

Hormann J. M. *Uniformen Der Infanterie,
1919 Bis Heute.* Friedberg, 1989

Joffre, Foch, Ludendorff et al *The Two
Battles of the Marne.* London, 1927

Jünger E. *The Storm of Steel.* London, 1929

Jünger E. *Copse 125.* London, 1930

Kaltenegger R. *Die Geschichte der
Deutschen Gebirgstruppe 1915 bis Heute.*
Stuttgart, 1980

Knappe S .& Brusaw E. *Soldat.*
Shrewsbury, 1993

Krawczyk W. *German Army Uniforms of
World War II.* London,1995

Lehmann R. *Die Leibstandarte.* English
trans. Winnipeg, 1988

Lucas J. *Experiences of War: The Third Reich.*
London, 1990

Lucas J. *Handbook of the German Army.*

BIBLIOGRAPHY

Stroud, 1998

Messenger C. *The Art of Blitzkrieg.*
London, 1990

Middlebrook M. *The Kaiser's Battle.*
London, 1978

Miksche F.O. *Blitzkrieg.* London, 1942

Mollo A. *German Uniforms of World War II.*
London, 1976

Mollo A. *Uniforms of the SS.* Collected edn.
London, 1997

Moyer L.V. *Victory Must be Ours: Germany
in the Great War.* London, 1995

Nash D. *German Infantry, 1914-1918.*
London, 1971

Necker W. *The German Army of Today.*
London, 1943

Nevin T. *Ernst Jünger and Germany.*
Duke University, 1996

Newton S.H. *German Battle Tactics on the
Eastern Front, 1941-1945.* Atglen, 1994

Pabst H. *The Outermost Frontier.*
London, 1957

Paschall R. *The Defeat of Imperial
Germany.* Chapel Hill, 1979

Patzwall K. D. *Deutsche Uniform und
Rang-Abzeichen 1933-1945.* Place not
given, 1980

Piekalkiewicz J. *Operation Citadel.* Novato,
1987

Pitt B. *1918: The Last Act.* London, 1962

Reibert W. *Der Dienst Unterricht im Heere.*
Berlin, 1936

Rommel E. *Infanterie Greift An.*
Potsdam, 1937

Rosciszewski L. *Niemiecke
Pancerzownice, Panzerschreck, Panzerfaust
1943-1945.* Warsaw, 1993

Rottman G. & Volstad R. *German Combat
Equipments.* London, 1991

SS Head Office *Dich Ruft die SS.*
Berlin, 1942

Samuels M. *Doctrine and Dogma:
German and British Infantry Tactics
in the First World War.* Westport, 1992

Scheibert H. & Wagener C. *Die Deutsche
Panzertruppe.* Bad Nauheim, 1966

Senich P.R. *The German Sniper.*
Boulder, 1982

Stahlberg A. *Bounden Duty.* London, 1990

Thomas N. & Andrew S. *The German
Army 1939 – 1945, Vol 1, Blitzkrieg.*
London, 1997

Walter J. *The German Rifle.* London, 1979

Walter J. *German Military Handguns
1879-1918.* London, 1980

Walter J. *The Luger Book.* London, 1986

War Department US *Handbook on
German Military Forces.* Washington, 1945

War Office Periodical Notes on the German
Army. No 18: *Schnelle T Truppen;
Reconnaissance; The Attack 1940.*
No 25: *Paramilitary forces 1940.*
No 36: *Tank tactics 1941.* No 40:
*Tactical handling of the armoured
division 1942.*

War Office *The German Army in Pictures*
various edns.

War Office *Handbook of the German Army.*
1940

War Office *Popular Guide to the German
Army. No 2: Infantry division 1941. No 4:
Engineers 1941.*

War Office *German Infantry in Action: Minor
Tactics.* 1941

War Office *The Regimental Officer's
Handbook of the German Army.* 1943

Wedd A.F. ed *German Students' War
Letters.* English edn. London, 1929

Weiß O. *Feldgrau in Krieg und Frieden.*
3 Vols. Berlin, 1916-1917

Wieder J. & von Einsiedel H.
Stalingrad Memories and Reassessments.
English edn. London, 1995

Zimmermann B. *Die Soldatenfibel.* Berlin,
c.1930

STORMTROOPER DIRECTORY

Museums

In the 1930s Germany boasted no less than 12 major public military museums, and several large collections within other museums. Though these have since been much reduced there remain several of interest. Currently the main venue is the Wehrgeschichtliches Museum, Karl Strasse 1, 7550, Rastatt, Germany. The main building of the Wehrgeschichtliches was the eighteenth century residence of the Margrave of Baden, and has subsequently served as the museum of the army of Baden, then as the military museum of South Western Germany, and, since 1969 as the museum of German military history, covering all periods from the middle ages to the present. Also worth noting is the Militarhistorisches Museum, Dr Kurt Fisher Platz 3, Dresden. The Bavarian army museum is located in the castle at Ingolstat. Be warned that those who seek out the military museum marked on old Munich street maps will find only a burned out shell...

In the UK, the Imperial War Museum, Lambeth Rd, London, SE1 6HZ, (0171 4165000) contains an unrivalled collection of German militaria, and the galleries devoted to the World Wars have undergone major refits in the last ten years. The museum also has research facilities which may be used by appointment. Latest news is that an outstation is planned for Manchester to add to those at Duxford Cambridgeshire, the Cabinet War Rooms, and HMS Belfast. German material is less well represented in British regimental museums, but scrutiny of T. & S. Wise's *Guide to Military Museums*, will undoubtedly pay dividends.

Elsewhere in Europe, the French Musée de l'Armee, Hotel Des Invalides, 75007, Paris, has useful material, as does the Belgian Army Museum, Parc Du Cinquantenaire 3, Brussels, which is particualrly strong on First World War German militaria. France and Belgium also have a good number of lesser collections concentrated on the battlefields of the First World War, on the Somme, Verdun and Ypres. A number of these, together with much useful battlefield information, will be found in R. Coombs' *Before Endeavours Fade*. There is

a cluster of small but interesting museums concentrating on the Second World War in Normandy. These include the Arromanches Musée du Débarquement and the Bayeux Musée de la Bataille de Normandie. A full listing will be found in W. G. Ramsay ed. D-Day Then and Now. Similarly there are several Ardennes related museums in eastern Belgium and Luxembourg. Significant amongst these are the Bastogne Historical Center; the La Gleize museum with its King Tiger; the Wiltz Castle Museum; and the Diekirch Museum which the local historical society have mounted within an old brewery.

Bookshops

There are many military history book dealers and publishers, some of whom are particularly strong on twentieth century German subjects. Not all operate from public outlets, and so a phone call or letter first is to be recommended. Noteworthy vendors include World of Warfare, 106 Browhead Rd, Burnley, Lancs, BB10 3BX 0128 – 420541; Paul Meekins Books, 34 Townsend Rd, Tiddington, Stratford-upon-Avon, Warwickshire, CV37 7DE (01789 295086) Chris Evans Books Freepost, Birmingham, B31 1BR (0121 4776700); Motor Books, 33 St Martin's Court, London, WC2N 4AL (0171 8365376) and 10 Theatre Square, Swindon, SN1 1QN (01793 523170). More generally useful, particularly for rare and antiquarian volumes, is Ken Trotman of Unit 11, 135 Ditton Walk, Cambridge, CB5 8PY (01223 211030). The main UK agent for Schiffer is Bushwood Books, 8 Marksbury Ave, Kew Gardens, Surrey, TW9 4JF. For those not about to spend a small fortune, the UK inter library loan system should not be forgotten – enquire at any public library. As far as magazines are concerned the best starting point in the UK is *Military Illustrated*. *Militaria* magazine, though sadly only availiable in French at present, is well worth investigation.

Re-enactment

With Second World War war crimes trials still in progress at the time of writing, and the reunification of Germany still recent,

re-enactment of German subjects can sometimes be viewed as questionable. Nevertheless it is an area of growing popularity outside Germany itself, and pursued to increasingly good standards by a number of groups. Many societies having now graduated from converted Swedish uniforms and other anachronisms and are using specially manufactured clothing of good quality, much of it from America. The US boasts many re-enactment societies including, 8 Gebirgsjäger Division, contact Mr P. Narzisi, 1136 Tulip St. Akron, OH, 44301; 9 Infanterie Division, contact Mr J.R. Penn 213 S. Oakley Ave., Mishawaka, IN 46544; 2 Panzer Division, contact Mr M. Smith, 7844 Ashbury Circle South, Hanover Park, IL, 60103.

In the UK a good starting point is the World War II Living History Association, 303 High St., Orpington, Kent, BR6 ONJ. The publicity officer for this association is Mr C. Leonard (01273 597093). Other groups of societies are covered by 'NAS', 22 Cousin Lane, Illingworth, Halifax, W. Yorks, HX2 8AF, and by Overlord Living History (01752 269544). Specific units of interest include 156 *Panzergrenadier Regiment* and its journal *Der Feldpost*, contact Mr P. Cadogan, 33 Peebles Close, Lindley, Huddersfield, HD3 3WD (01484 317387). In Wales the contact for *Fallschirmjäger Regiment 6* is Mr R Mardle (01650 521371). In the Midlands military police are represented by *Feldgendarmerie Abt. 66*, contact Mr I Vaughn (01926 497593). The *Grossdeutschland Citadel* Society may be reached via Mr D. Choules, 15 Mill Walk, Whitwell, Worksop, Notts, S80 4SH (01909 723297). Further south the Second Battle Group contact is Mr A. Colbourn, 159 Downsway, Southwick, W. Sussex, BN 42 4WF; and for *916 Grenadier Regiment* Mr A. Dudman PO Box 156 Loughton, Essex, GR10 1TY. The reconstruction of First World War units is arguably more difficult, given the passage of time, yet there are a number of groups doing re-enactment of the period. These include the specifically relevant *Sturmkompagnie* of The Flanders Society, contact Mr R. Matthews, 26A Old School Close, Burwell, Cambs, CB5 OAS.

INDEX

APPENDIX

WAFFENFARBEN: ARM OF SERVICE COLOURS

In 1914 shoulder strap pipings usually distinguished the Army Corps of a unit , but in September 1915 a new colour system to denote arm of service was introduced. The basic colours were,

Troop Type	Strap piping	Body of strap
Infantry	White	Field grey
Jäger and Schützen	Light green	Grey green
Garde Schützen	Black	Grey green
Cavalry	Various	Various
Pioneers	Scarlet	Black
Medical troops	Cornflower blue	Dark blue

As used during the National Socialist era, Waffenfarbe was a highly developed colour coding to categorise a mass of different unit types. It appeared not only as a shoulder strap piping, but as an inverted chevron of colour on the peakless Feldmütze, as piping on the dress cap or Schirmmutze, and on certain types of uniform was a feature of the Litzen and collar decoration. Despite simplifications it continued to be used, at least on shoulder straps, until 1945.

Waffenfarben applied to the Army included :

Hochrot	(Bright red)	Generals and artillery
Bordorot	(Bordeaux red)	Smoke / rocket troops
Rosa	(Rose pink)	Armour
Orangerot	(Orange)	Field police and recruiters
Karmesin	(Carmine)	Veterinary troops
Weisse	(White)	Infantry
Goldgelb	(Golden yellow)	Cavalry
Zitronengelb	(Lemon yellow)	Signals
Kupferbraun	(Copper brown)	Motorised reconnaisance
Hellgrün	(Light green)	Mountain troops
Weisengrün	(Grass green)	Armoured infantry
Dunkelgrün	(Dark green)	Administrative officials
Hellblau	(Light blue)	Transport troops
Dunkelblau	(Dark blue)	Medical personnel
Schwarz	(Black)	Pioneers
Schwarzweiss	(Black and white)	Armoured engineers
Hellgrau	(Light grey)	Propaganda troops

During World War Two the Waffen SS Waffenfarben were essentially the same, though on caps the SS dispensed with arm of service colours and used white piping from December 1940. Certain additional colours were also used by the SS :

Hellbraun	(Light brown)	Concentration camp guards
Hell-Lachrosa	(Light pink)	Military geologists
Dunkelgrau	(Dark grey)	Reichsführer personal staff
Rotgrau	(Red and grey)	Fachführer specialists
Lichtblau	(Light sky blue)	Administration

RANKS OF THE ARMY AND SS

Other Ranks:

Army	Waffen SS
Schütze; Grenadier	Schütze; Grenadier
Oberschütze	Oberschütze
Gefreiter	Sturmmann
Obergefreiter	Rottenführer
Unteroffizier	Unterscharführer
Fahnenjunker	Junker
Unterfeldwebel	Scharführer
Fähnrich	Standartenjunker
Feldwebel	Oberscharführer
Oberfeldwebel	Hauptscharführer
Oberfähnrich	Standarten-Oberjunker
Stabsfeldwebel	Sturmscharführer

Officers:

Army	Waffen SS
Leutnant	Untersturmführer
Oberleutnant	Obersturmführer
Hauptmann	Hauptsturmführer
Major	Sturmbannführer
Oberstleutnant	Obersturmbannführer
Oberst	Standartenführer, Oberführer
Generalmajor	Brigadeführer
Generalleutnant	Gruppenführer
General	Obergruppenführer
Generaloberst	Oberstgruppenführer

ACKNOWLEDGEMENTS

A number of people have helped to make this book possible. I should especially like to thank the staffs of the Imperial War Museum library and photo library, and Lancashire County Libraries; Tim Newark with whom the original concept was developed; Anya Sprenz for her help with the German language; Ted Neville of TRH Pictures, and Alan Beadle who supplied many of the original artifacts. The reconstruction team which served well beyond the call of duty was Adrian Warrall; Lawrence Becket; Graham Lund, and photographer Mike Seed.